YOU ASKED?

**Over 300 Great Questions
and Astounding Answers**

YOU ASKED?

Over 300 Great Questions and Astounding Answers

From the Editors of OWL Magazine

Compiled and Edited by Katherine Farris

Owl Books

Owl Books are published by Greey de Pencier Books Inc.,
70 The Esplanade, Suite 400, Toronto, ON, Canada M5E 1R2

OWL Magazine is an award-winning science and nature publication for children 8 and up.
For more information or to subscribe, send a letter with your name and address to
OWL, 179 John Street, Suite 500, Toronto, Ontario, Canada M5T 3G5.
In the United States, contact OWL, 25 Boxwood Lane, Buffalo NY 14227-2780.

Distributed in the United States by Firefly Books (U.S.) Inc.,
230 Fifth Avenue, Suite 1607, New York, NY 10001.

This book was published with the generous support of the Canada Council, the Ontario Arts Council
and the Ontario Publishing Centre.

Canadian Cataloguing in Publication Data

Main entry under title:

You asked? : Over 300 great questions and astounding answers

Includes index.
ISBN 1-895688-58-2 (bound) ISBN 1-895688-59-0 (pbk.)

1. Science – Miscellanea – Juvenile literature.
I. Farris, Katherine.

Q163.Y68 1996 j500   C95-932572-7

Design & Art Direction: Wycliffe Smith, Julie Colantonio, Julia Naimska
Cover Photo Illustration © Bob Anderson

Printed in Hong Kong

D   E   F

TABLE OF CONTENTS

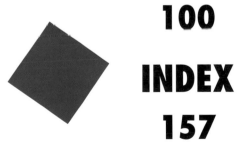

YOU ASKED?

Have you ever wondered *why* something is the way it is or *how* something happens? Are you full of questions about everyday things that no one can answer? Then this book's for you. It's packed with answers to hundreds of questions about high-tech stuff (like lasers and fireworks), low-tech stuff (like ski wax and bicycle tires), space, animals, plants, and — in this first section — even your own body.

But before you get to the answers, here's a question for you. What can bend and twist, feel firm and soft, be fuzzy and smooth, feel pain and pleasure, make noise on the inside and stay silent on the outside, all at the same time? If you guessed the human body, you're right. You might feel you know your body well, but chances are you've wondered about it, too. For instance, do you have big ear lobes or small ones, and why? If your ears hang low and wobble to and fro, the gene for big ear lobes was passed on to you by one or both of your parents. Genes are the instructions that your body followed as it first developed. They determine things like the color of your eyes and the size of your ear lobes.

Genes partly determine how hairy you are, but why doesn't hair grow on the palms of your hands and the soles of your feet? Hair on your palms and soles would trap heat that your sweat glands need to release, and it would cushion nerve endings that connect to your brain and give you your sense of touch. Hair would also cover up the tiny ridges of skin that act like treads to keep you from losing your grip or your step. So it's a good thing your bare feet are really bare!

Speaking of feet, have you ever noticed that some feet smell like stinky cheese? That smell is from bacteria that live on your body and like to eat sweat. Since there are nearly 200,000 sweat pores on every square inch (2.5 cm^2) of your soles, bacteria love your feet! When your feet smell like strong cheese, it's because bacteria are digesting substances that are found both in sweat and in the milk curds that bacteria ripen into cheese.

If all this talk about cheese has made you hungry, maybe you're salivating. What does saliva do? It tells you if your lunch is "mouth-watering" good by softening and moistening the food so your taste buds can taste it. Saliva also helps digest food with a chemical called an enzyme. You won't run out of saliva, because glands under your tongue make a constant supply. Just thinking about food can put these glands into action. They make about 550 ml (2 cups) of saliva every day. Smart mouth!

Speaking of smarts, ever wonder how much your brain weighs? When you were born, your brain weighed about as much as a large orange. By the time you're full grown, it will be about as hefty as a cantaloupe.

So put your brain to work on how x-rays work. Objects cast shadows where they block the sun's rays. X-rays have much shorter waves than sunlight, and aren't so easy to stop. They pass right through skin, blood and muscles to mark a piece of special film. Bones are dense, and block enough x-rays to cast a shadow on the film. Organs are dense enough to block some x-rays, leaving cloudier shadows than bones, and letting doctors get to know their patients inside out.

If you're keen to learn more about yourself, inside and out, just turn the page. You'll find lots more questions and answers to help you understand the mystery and wonder that is you.

Why do you wake up? ▷

It's the weekend and you don't need to get up early. So why do you wake up on a sleep-in Saturday the same time you wake up on school days? Your internal "alarm clock" tells you it's time to wake up. But what sets your "alarm clock" to go off? Sunlight does. If you lived totally in the dark your internal clock would run slower and slower until you ended up sleeping and waking at very odd times. But sunlight resets your clock every day, so you operate on a more-or-less 24-hour schedule – just like the planet you live on.

Why does sunshine make you feel good?

When you wake up on a sunny day, getting up seems easy. Why? Sunlight, especially early morning light, helps to keep your body's biological rhythm in line. And when your body's rhythm is "in beat," you feel good. Most people aren't really aware how much they need sunlight until they get the short dark days of fall and winter. Then the lack of sunlight can be a real problem for some people. It causes their biological rhythm to go haywire and they become sleepy, cranky and sad. But scientists have found that exposing these people daily to bright light helps to keep them alert and happy.

Why do people get thirsty?

If you feel thirsty it's because you've lost more water than you've taken in. How do you lose water? By sweating and by elimination. Your body needs lots of water and it will let you know if you should drink up. How? Thirst receptors in the back of your throat dry up and make you feel parched. When this happens your brain sends out the message, "Hey, drink up!"

Salty foods can also make you feel thirsty. Why? Salt absorbs water. When you cram a handful of chips into your mouth, the salt on them dries out your thirst receptors, leaving you with that familiar dry-mouthed feeling. Once you've taken a drink of something you'll feel better. That is, of course, until you cram in the next handful of chips.

What makes your stomach growl?

Next time you're sitting in a quiet classroom just before lunch, listen for the sound of growling stomachs. Doctors call this "borborygmi," which sounds a bit like the noise you hear. It happens when your stomach walls automatically squeeze together in an attempt to mix and digest food and there's no food there. Gases and digestive juices slosh around inside your empty stomach and before you know it . . . borborygmi, borborygmi.

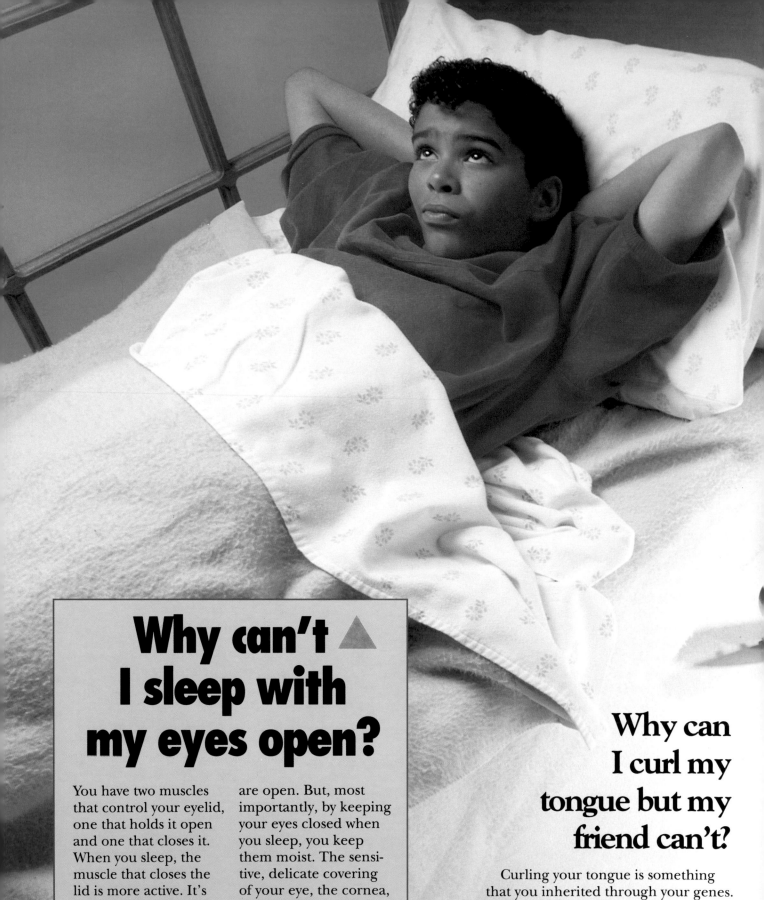

Why can't ◢ I sleep with my eyes open?

You have two muscles that control your eyelid, one that holds it open and one that closes it. When you sleep, the muscle that closes the lid is more active. It's a good thing, too. Your brain needs a break from the endless flow of pictures it has to process while your eyes are open. But, most importantly, by keeping your eyes closed when you sleep, you keep them moist. The sensitive, delicate covering of your eye, the cornea, needs to be constantly moistened by tears. If it dries out, you won't be able to see.

Why can I curl my tongue but my friend can't?

Curling your tongue is something that you inherited through your genes. Check out your family. Can either or both of your parents curl their tongues? How about your grandparents? Someone among your ancestors was able to perform this trick and they passed it on to you.

Why do we have wax in our ears?

You may not like having wax in your ears, but it's there for a good reason — it keeps your ears in good working order.

Wax is produced by glands near the eardrum and continually washes away down the ear canal. One of the most important things wax does is protect the eardrum from bacteria. It also keeps the eardrum moist and pliable so that it can respond to different sounds.

And if that's not enough to make you glad about wax, then what about this? Earwax also prevents dust and bugs from getting stuck in your ears!

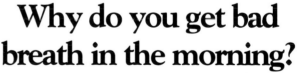

Why do you get bad breath in the morning?

Bad breath is a reminder that your body is active even as you sleep. During the night, your stomach churns because you haven't eaten for a while. Smelly stomach gases rise up through your throat. When you open your mouth the next morning — jungle breath! Also as you sleep, skin inside your mouth that's slowly rubbed away hangs around and creates smelly fumes. And if you forgot to brush your teeth the night before, decaying food will also cause bad breath.

Why does your hair stand on end when you get cold or scared? ▼

When you get really scared, your nervous system sends adrenaline through your body to give you more energy. Adrenaline also makes your heart beat faster, your muscles contract and your hair stand on end. Bristly hair is especially important for an animal that's trying to scare off a predator. It makes the animal look much bigger and more ferocious. Bristly hair doesn't really help you when you're scared, but it does when it's cold. The upright hairs trap a thicker layer of air next to your skin and this insulates you better.

How does mousse keep your hair in place?

Mousse works by "gluing" your hair together. Feel your hair after moussing it and you'll know what we mean. It's the resin in mousse that makes it so sticky. (Yes, the same stuff that gives bubble gum extra stretch.) When you style a curl or wave into your hair, the resin binds the hairs together in that shape so they will all bounce back into place if they get tousled. It's almost as if the resin makes your hair remember the style you've given it. Mousse also makes your hair look thicker and fuller because it contains proteins similar to the proteins in your hair. The resin binds these proteins to your hair, making each hair shaft thicker – until you wash the mousse out.

Why does head hair grow longer than other hair?

Hairs have a natural life-span. The hairs on your head live longer than your other hairs. They grow for about two to five years before they fall out. Eyelashes, on the other hand, only last for about four months. Just imagine what would happen if your eyelashes grew as long as your hair!

How many hairs are there on a person's head?

You have about 100,000 head hairs and each one grows approximately 0.25 mm/100th of an inch a day. That may not seem like much, but if you added up the daily growth of all your hairs it would total 25 m/1,000 inches. You won't become too hairy, though, because you lose about 50 head hairs a day. That's more than 18,000 a year! Good thing they don't all fall out at once.

Why does a hot curling-iron curl your hair?

When you heat your hair with a curling-iron, you can go from straight hair to a headful of curls in just a few minutes. Why? Heat causes chains of protein molecules inside each hair to start to vibrate and pull apart. The hair then "softens" in much the same way as a sheet of plastic will soften when heated. And, like the plastic, if you shape your hair when it's soft, then let it cool, it will "harden" into the new shape. A curling-iron not only heats your hair to soften it, but it also shapes your hair into a curl.

Why do we have hair?

Millions of years ago people needed hair to keep warm. Even though you now wear clothes for warmth, you still need your hair. Eyebrows and eyelashes keep dirt out of your eyes. Head hair helps to insulate your brain from extreme temperatures. And the hair on your body acts as an early warning system to detect insects that are about to land.

Why does it hurt to pull your hair but not to cut it?

Getting your hair cut doesn't hurt because the part that is cut is dead and can't "feel." It'll only hurt if your hair dresser accidentally pulls your hair. The hair below the skin is alive, and it's attached to nerves. When hair is pulled, the nerves send a pain message to your brain. Ouch!

Why does hair turn gray as people get older?

You may be surprised to learn that there's no such thing as gray hair. So why does your aunt look like she has gray hair, while your grandmother is crowned with a snow-white head of hair? Believe it or not, hair looks gray because pure white hairs are mixed in with colored ones. And the reason people get more white hairs as they get older is because they stop producing melanin, the substance that gives hair its color.

How can a boy tell if he'll go bald?

Nobody's really sure why people go bald, but some scientists believe that you may inherit baldness. If you're interested, check out your mother's father. Your hairline may look like his when you get older.

Why do eyes sometimes look red in photos?

If all your photographs turn your friends into red-eye fiends, take heart. What you've done is aimed your flash directly into their eyes. When the light flashes, you capture on film a very neat photo of the inside of everyone's eyeballs. They're red because they contain lots of blood vessels. To avoid that wild-eyed look on future photos, either tell your friends to look slightly away from the flash or, if possible, hold the flashgun off to the side and then click.

Do blind people dream?

Yes. Blind people who could once see can still "see" in their dreams. But people who have been blind from birth have dreams with no pictures. Their dreams are full of smell, taste, touch and sound sensations.

What's wrong with your eyes if you're color blind?

Being color blind only affects how you see colors, not how well you see. People with full color vision have three types of cone-shaped cells in their eyes. One type of cone sees red light, another green and the third blue. A color blind person is missing one or more types of cones. Red-green color blindness is the most common and occurs when the red or green cones are absent. People with this type of color blindness see red or green as gray-brown. Here's a test for red-green color blindness. What number do you see in this group of dots?
(Answer: If you saw the number 15, then you have normal color vision. If you saw the number 17, you may have red-green color blindness.)

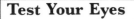
Test Your Eyes

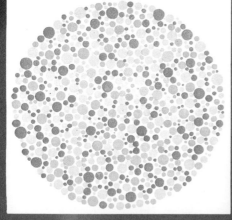

Why can't you lift your ring finger when you curl your middle finger under?

It's all a question of tendons. Try this trick. Place your hand on a table in the position shown in the photo.

Try to lift your ring finger. No matter how hard you try, you won't be able to do it. Why? Because the tendons of

the middle and ring finger are joined together. When you prevent the middle finger from moving

by bending it under, your ring finger can't move either.

Why do you have lines, ridges and swirls on your fingertips?

No matter how young you are, your fingertips and palms are covered with lines and ridges. But don't worry, you need them. They give you a better grip, like the treads on tires. Smooth fingertips would slither off things you're trying to pick up. Prove it by sticking smooth tape over the fingertips of your thumb and index finger. Now try to pick up a piece of paper or a dime or turn the pages of this book . . .

How do artificial hands work?

In this photograph, Jennifer Schoenhals is using a myo-electric hand — a battery-operated artificial hand that she controls with a miniature computer. The computer uses electrical signals from the muscles in her lower arm to tell the hand to open and close, similar to the way your hand works. A gentle muscle contraction closes the hand and a strong one opens it. Her myoelectric hand is easy to remove, so she can quickly switch to her special "swimming" hand, "gymnastics" hand or whatever special-use hand she needs.

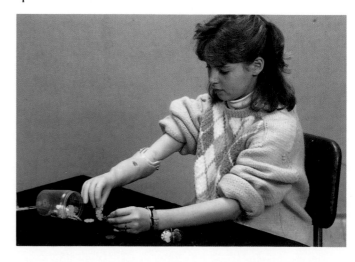

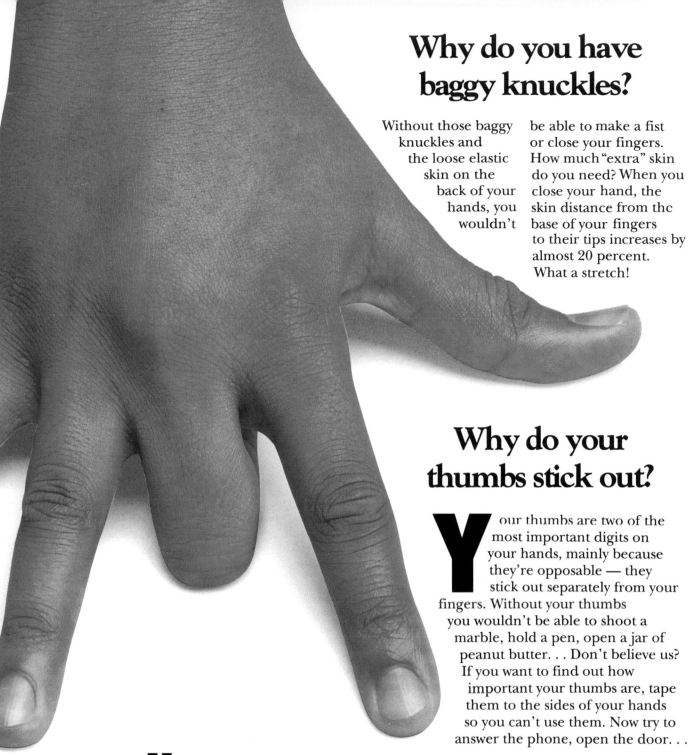

Why do you have baggy knuckles?

Without those baggy knuckles and the loose elastic skin on the back of your hands, you wouldn't be able to make a fist or close your fingers. How much "extra" skin do you need? When you close your hand, the skin distance from the base of your fingers to their tips increases by almost 20 percent. What a stretch!

Why do your thumbs stick out?

Your thumbs are two of the most important digits on your hands, mainly because they're opposable — they stick out separately from your fingers. Without your thumbs you wouldn't be able to shoot a marble, hold a pen, open a jar of peanut butter. . . Don't believe us? If you want to find out how important your thumbs are, tape them to the sides of your hands so you can't use them. Now try to answer the phone, open the door. . .

How come fingers are so strong when they're so small and skinny?

Drum your fingers on a table or "play" the piano in the air. See the "cords" moving in the backs of your hands? Those cords are your tendons, and they attach your muscles to your bones. The tendons in your hands carry muscle power all the way from your elbow to your fingers. So although your fingers might be small and slender, they're backed up by a lot of power.

What's a nose for?

Your nose does a lot more than just take up space between your eyes. Not only does it bring in air and let you smell and taste things; it also prepares the air for your lungs by warming it up. The hairs in your nose – the ones you can see as well as microscopic ones – filter the air and prevent particles from entering your lungs. And your nose also acts as an echo chamber to give your voice its unique sound.

Why does sniffing hard help you smell better?

If someone gave you a rose, what would be the first thing you'd do? You'd probably sniff it. Usually when you breathe, not much air moves up to the very top of your nose where your smell cells are. But when you sniff you breathe in a lot more air and you aim it right at your nose's smell center.

Why do noses run?

Your nose is always producing mucus, but sometimes it makes too much. Then it's quick, pass the tissues! When you cry your nose runs because some of your tears drip down overflow tubes that connect your eyes to your nose. Your nose also runs to flush out dirt and germs.

Why can't you taste anything when you've got a cold?

You're tired, your eyes are sore and when your nose isn't running it's all stuffed up. That's right: you've got a cold. And one of the worst things about having a cold is that your tongue feels funny and everything tastes like cardboard. Why? Because your nose is full of gooey mucus and no air can reach your smell cells. And that's where the trouble lies. Without your sense of smell you can hardly taste the difference between foul-tasting medicine and chocolate milk.

What's the loudest hiccup ever heard?

According to the Guinness Book of World Records, in 1769 a man from Long Witton, Northumberland, suffered from hiccups that could be heard more than 1.6 km/ 1 mi away!

Hic Hiccup Hiccup Hic Hic

What's the quietest hiccup?

Babies can get the hiccups — even before they're born. Pregnant mothers have reported hearing hiccups only to discover that the sound was coming from inside them!

What happens when you get the hiccups?

It's probably happened to you. You're sitting in a quiet classroom and all of a sudden HICC! And then another. HICC! Hiccup after hiccup, and there's nothing you can do, because hiccups are one of those things you can't control. To understand why, you need to know about the workings of your diaphragm.

Your diaphragm is a dome-shaped muscle that stretches across your body between your lungs and stomach. When this powerful muscle contracts, it reduces the air pressure in your lungs so air gets pulled into them — and you inhale. You exhale when your diaphragm relaxes and air is forced out of your lungs. You get an attack of the hiccups when your diaphragm stops behaving normally and goes into a muscle spasm. Being cold can trigger a spasm, and so can having an over-full stomach. Eating and drinking too much can overstretch your stomach so that it presses against your diaphragm. This triggers electrical signals from the nerve that controls the movement of your diaphragm, causing a sudden spasm. Talking while you're eating can also force extra air into your stomach with the same result. So, one way to avoid the hiccups is not to talk with your mouth full.

What's the longest anyone's had the hiccups?

Charles Osborne of Iowa has had the hiccups for more than 60 years. That's approximately 420 million hiccups.

Why do I have a groove connecting my top lip and my nose? ▼

You might not believe this, but that groove is part of a double seam where three pieces of your face joined together. It happened while you were a developing baby inside your mom, and it's visible proof that all your muscles and other soft tissue started growing from your backbone and joined together at your front. On your head, three pieces of facial tissue – two big ones from your cheeks and a smaller one from your nose – met at the center of your top lip. When they fused, the build-up of tissue formed a double seam with a little groove in between. The groove is called the "philtrum." Check out other people's philtra – they come in all shapes and sizes. Just don't stare too long – it's rude!

What causes a "stitch" in your side?

Doctors think the sharp pain you call a stitch sometimes comes when gas builds up after you eat too much. Or it might be caused by a sore diaphragm. This large muscle pushes air in and out of your lungs. The faster you run, the harder it works. When your diaphragm tires, it begins to hurt. That's when you feel a stitch in your side.

Why do my ears pop when I go up in a fast elevator?

That popping sound you hear is your eardrums snapping back after they've bulged out of place. But why do they bulge? When you go up in a really fast elevator, the air pressure outside your ears drops quickly. But the pressure inside your ears doesn't change as fast, resulting in uneven pressure on your eardrums. Groan! To even up the pressure, try swallowing. This opens up the small tube that connects the back of your mouth to the inside of your ears and reduces the pressure by releasing trapped air. Pop!

What's the most powerful muscle in the human body?

Believe it or not, the most powerful muscle you possess is attached to your head. No, it's not your tongue – it's your jaw muscle. This may surprise you, but it shouldn't. Muscles get stronger by being used. And your jaw muscle gets a lot of exercise.

How many bones do I have in my body? When you were born, you had about 250 bones. Now you only have about 206. What happened? You haven't actually lost any bones. It's just that some of your bones, such as the ones in your face, have fused together. By the time you're your parents' age you'll only have about 200 bones. Read on, and bone up on some amazing bone facts.

How many bones are in your head?

One, right? Wrong! The helmet of bone that protects your brain is actually seven bones that fit together like the pieces of a jigsaw puzzle.

What's the biggest bone in your body?

The biggest bone in your body is the thigh-bone or femur, the one that connects the hip-bone to the knee-bone. It's got to be big and strong to support your weight as well as all the leg muscles that are attached to it. And it's long so that you can take big strides when you're walking.

What's inside your bones?

Bones account for one-fifth of your total weight. But even though they are light-weight and can flex, they are strong enough to support you. Your bones are made up of two layers. On the outside is "compact" bone, which is thick and dense, rather like ivory. It sets the shape of the bone and anchors the muscles. The next layer is made up of "cancellous" bone, an intricate girder-like mesh. This lattice-like, honey-combed network is very light but, ounce for ounce, it is stronger than steel.

Running throughout the cancellous bone are little "canals" that carry veins, arteries, cells and fluid which keep the bones strong and healthy. In the core of your bones is mar-row. Marrow makes red blood cells and provides your body with an energy reserve.

What's the tiniest bone in your body?

The smallest bone in your body is in your ear. It's called the stirrup bone. Here it is. You can see how it got its name.

What keeps your bones to-gether?

Stretchy straps called ligaments tie your bones together so they don't slip out of place, but not so tight that they can't move.

Can ribs move?

The bony cage that protects your heart and lungs looks rigid but it's not. Your rib cage is loosely joined to your backbone so that the ribs can move outward. If they didn't, you wouldn't be able to breathe.

How can you keep your brain from getting rusty?

In some ways brains are like cars. Some are like Ferraris — they are very sophisticated and can go very fast. Others are more like Volkswagens — slow but sure. But no matter what kind of car (or brain) you have, if you keep it well-oiled you'll get the maximum mileage out of it. And you won't have to worry about "rust."

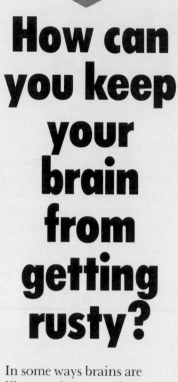

How you "oil" your brain depends on you. Some people keep their brains from rusting by doing math, others by reading.

What's important is to keep doing whatever it is you're interested in. Why? Your brain is a very complex circuit that runs on electrical impulses. The more inter-connections between the brain's cells, the better the circuit works. Scientists think that by practicing a task over and over again you help your brain to create new connections that are specifically made for that task. So instead of having to take a long, circuitous route through your brain, the impulse travels along a short and specific path. The more you practice, the better and faster you'll be.

Help stop your brain from getting rusty by trying this quiz.

Body Quiz

You scratch it, feed it, sleep in it and take it to school. But how much do you really know about your body?

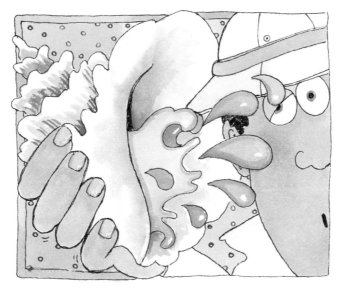

1 The largest organ in your body is your:
a) brain
b) big toe
c) skin

2 The air you expel in a sneeze travels about as fast as:
a) a cheetah
b) a hurricane-force wind
c) the speed of sound

3 If all the blood vessels in your body were laid end to end, they'd stretch:
a) from Toronto to New York
b) across the Atlantic Ocean
c) around the world

4 Your body contains the same amount of iron as:
a) a steam iron
b) an iron frying pan
c) a small iron nail

5 The time of day when you're the tallest is:
a) before breakfast
b) at lunch time
c) after dinner

6 The sound you hear when you put a seashell to your ear is:
a) waves breaking on Waikiki Beach
b) a secret message from a shrimp
c) the echo of blood moving in your ear

7 During your lifetime you'll likely eat the equivalent weight of:
a) 3 elephants
b) 6 elephants
c) 12 elephants

8 Your heart is about the same size as your:
a) eyeball
b) fist
c) head

9 The hardest substance in your body is found in your:
a) thigh bone
b) spine
c) teeth

10 If your skin could be stretched flat it would cover about the same area as a:
a) postage stamp
b) towel
c) billiard table

11 When you blush, another part of your body that turns red is:
a) the lining of your stomach
b) your hair
c) your anklebone

12 Your brain is mostly made of:
a) muscle
b) water
c) mysterious matter from outer space

13 If all the nerves in your body were placed end to end they'd stretch:
a) from Toronto to New York
b) across the Atlantic Ocean
c) around the world

Check your answers and give yourself one point for each correct answer. Then find out how you rate as a body brain.

■ 0-5: You do have a body, don't you?

■ 6-10: You're nobody's fool!

■ 11-13: You're really a some-body!

Answers:
1. c; 2. b; 3. b; 4. c; 5. a;
6. c; 7. b; 8. b; 9. c; 10. c;
11. a; 12. b; 13. b.

What's a scab?

Skateboarders call scabs pavement pizzas, but you might prefer to think of them as bandages your blood makes. Here's why. When you scratch or cut yourself, cells in your blood instantly start a two-part patching process. They stick around the edges of the cut to help plug up the wound and at the same time produce a substance that makes a protein called fibrin. When seen through a microscope, fibrin looks like strands of spaghetti. As the strands form, they interweave and slowly pull together the sides of the wound. Blood cells get trapped between the fibrin strands, turning the scab dark red.

Why does it hurt so much when you hit your funny bone?

The funny thing about your funny bone is that it's not a bone at all. What you're really hitting is your ulnar nerve, the nerve that carries messages to and from your brain and fingers. Most of your nerves are well protected by skin and flesh. But for some reason — and scientists aren't sure why — your ulnar nerve doesn't have much padding where it passes through your elbow. So when you bump your elbow, you often hit the nerve — OUCH! Not only does it really hurt, it also sends that weird tingly feeling to your fingers.

Why do bruises start off black and end up yellow?

Ouch! You bruise yourself when you break tiny blood vessels beneath your skin. But your body soon repairs the damage. Within minutes blood vessels reseal and clean-up cells arrive to break down and carry away the dead, leaked blood cells. This blood looks black and so your new bruise looks black. As more dead blood cells are removed, the bruise gets lighter in color and looks blue. After a few black-and-blue days your bruise looks green because some molecules in the dead blood turn green as they're broken down. As more of those molecules are carted away, your bruise turns lighter green or yellow, until it disappears.

Why does it hurt to bend your knee after you've scraped it?

Once you've scraped your knee it will start to scab. Not only does a scab look different from the rest of your skin, it also isn't as stretchy and elastic. So when you bend your knee, the scab doesn't stretch. Instead it pulls against the sensitive edges of the scraped area. And that hurts!

Why do you get a headache when you eat ice cream too fast? ▶

Inside your hard palate – in the roof of your mouth – is a nerve that connects with your forehead. When you eat ice cream quickly, your brain receives a message that some part of your face is getting chilled too fast for comfort. Even though it doesn't know whether it's your forehead or your hard palate that's in trouble, it responds by sending back a pain alert. And yes, you guessed it. Your forehead intercepts the message and ends up with the pain. Think of that the next time you gobble down a triple scoop chocolate fudge delight!

Does eating chocolate cause pimples?

Pimples are caused by bacteria. And these bacteria seem to thrive on oil. If you eat foods that are high in oil and fat, such as chocolate, you increase your production of oil. And more oil on your skin is just what pimple-causing bacteria enjoy. Skin specialists report that some of their patients say they break out in pimples after eating certain foods, including chocolate. But don't just blame chocolate. If you have a problem with pimples you should try to avoid any other oil producing and fat foods or foods with a high sugar content. You should also stay away from any other food that causes you problems. Other than eating a healthy diet, is there anything else you can do? If your face is greasy you should wash it two or three times a day with soap and avoid greasy make-up. Now where have you heard all that before?

Why do you itch?

An itch is a warning that there's something on your skin that shouldn't be there. This could be an insect or something you're allergic to, even sunshine. Some scientists think the itch signal travels along pain nerves to your brain, which would make an itch a mini-pain. Others think the itch signal travels along nerves reserved especially for itches. No matter how the message gets to your brain, your natural reaction is to scratch...

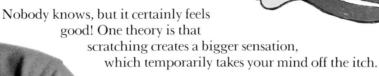

Does scratching stop an itch?

Nobody knows, but it certainly feels good! One theory is that scratching creates a bigger sensation, which temporarily takes your mind off the itch.

If your skin is always renewing itself, how can you have a scar for life?

The outer part of your skin, the epidermis, renews itself once every 28 days. It's made up of cells that keep pushing up towards the surface, where they die and are rubbed off by your clothing or in the shower. A scar forms when the epidermis and the layer of skin just below it are injured and replaced by scar tissue. This scar tissue is much tougher than normal and doesn't produce new cells like the surrounding tissue. That means the scar never changes and never gets rubbed off like other used-up skin cells.

Why are most people right-handed?

No one really knows for sure, but it was once thought that it was an advantage for ancient warriors to be right-handed. Why?
A right-handed warrior would hold his spear in his right hand, leaving his left hand free to hold his shield over the left side of his body, and thus protect his heart. Today scientists have thrown out this theory. They now know that handedness is decided in the brain, but they still haven't solved the mystery of why nine out of ten people are right-handed.

Are people left-footed too?

If you're left-handed you're probably left-footed too. And if you're right-handed you probably favor your right foot.

Here's a quick test to find out.

Which foot do you use to kick a ball?
Right ☐   Left ☐

Take off your shoes and socks and pick up a pencil with your toes. Which do you automatically use?
Right ☐   Left ☐
If you used the same foot for both things, that's the foot you prefer. If you had two different answers, you may not have a preference. Does this make you ambipedrous?

Are we born right- or left-handed?

Babies seem to use both hands, but they do have a favorite side. And scientists have found that the hand on the favorite side usually ends up being the preferred hand. To predict which hand a baby will favor when she grows up, watch which side she usually faces when lying on her back. If it's to the right, the baby will probably be right-handed and vice versa.

Are lefties better at doing certain things?

Some people (probably lefties) claim that left-handed people are more creative and also may do better at subjects requiring logic, such as mathematics. What scientists know for sure is that lefties are better baseball hitters than righties. Scientists think that's because even though left-handers favor their left, they're pretty good with their right too. So they have two good hands on the bat.

Can some people use both hands?

Yes. A few people are ambidextrous. That means they can use either hand to do the same task. But that's very rare. Other people are mixed-handed – they can do different tasks with different hands.

Why does it hurt when you laugh really hard?

When someone tells you a joke and you start to laugh really hard, you tense up your stomach muscles and pump your diaphragm up and down. If you keep on laughing you end up with over-exercised stomach and diaphragm muscles – and they hurt! But just think.

Some people get the same kind of soreness by doing push-ups. At least it's more fun to laugh.

Why does laughing make you feel good?

Believe it or not, laughter is basically a tension release mechanism. When your body feels tense, it seeks a way to get rid of its tension. Exercise is one way, but laughter is equally effective. And once the tension is gone you feel better.

Why do people burp?

People burp because they've swallowed air. Sometimes people take huge gulps of air when they eat – for instance when they swallow soup and try to cool it at the same time.

Other times, there's lots of air in what they're eating or drinking – for example, soda pop. When the carbon dioxide is released in the stomach, the air comes up, bubbles over the back of the throat and – oops, excuse me!

Why do your eyes cry when you're laughing really hard?

Take a close look at someone who's laughing really hard. Their face is all squeezed up and their mouth is probably wide open. If you took a picture and showed it to a friend, your friend probably wouldn't be able to tell if the person was laughing or yawning. Your eyes "cry" when you laugh, just as they "cry" when you yawn. Why? That squeezed-up face puts pressure on the tear glands. If the glands are full, tears will drop out.

What is personal space?

◆ Just as animals have their territories to defend, so do people. Personal space is the space immediately surrounding you that you claim as your own. If anyone gets too close to you under the wrong circumstances, you feel uncomfortable because your personal space has been invaded.

Why do you have personal space?

Scientists still aren't sure why people have personal spaces. One idea is that it keeps you from bumping into people or having things spilled on you. Or perhaps keeping your distance helps slow down the spread of germs.

How big is your personal space?

If you could see your personal space, it would probably look something like a bulky spacesuit. It's a bit bigger in front of you than at your sides or behind you.

Whom you're with, where you are and what you're doing all help determine the size of your personal space. It "shrinks" when you're with people you like and trust.

How to find out the size of your personal space

1. In an open area, ask a friend to stand 2 m/7 ft away, facing you.

2. Tell her to look at your chin and walk slowly towards you, hands at her sides. She mustn't grin or make a face.

3. You should look at her eyes. When you feel uncomfortable about how close she is getting, say "stop."

4. Ask other friends to approach you in the same way. To find out your average personal space, divide the sum of all the distances by the number of people who approached you.

5. Ask your friends to do the same to find their average personal space.

Does your personal space change when you can't see?

Repeat the experiment that tests the size of your personal space, but blindfold yourself. As in the first experiment, have several kids approach you. The approachers must count as they walk towards you so you know where they are. Tell them to stop when you feel uncomfortable and measure the distance between you. Record these distances, then figure out your average "blindfolded" personal space. Is it different from the average with your eyes open? Ask the other kids to test their average "blindfolded" personal space.

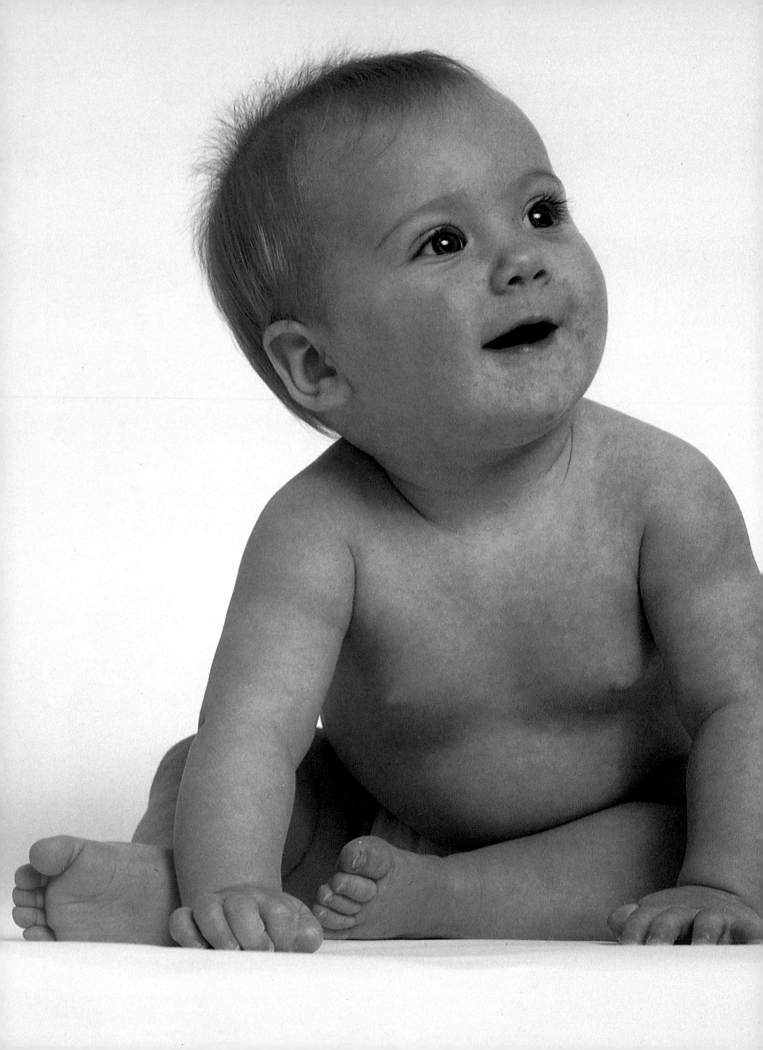

Why are babies so cute?

Babies' looks are designed to help them get what they want. That might sound strange to you, but since babies can't talk, they need other ways to tell their parents what they want or need. For example, a baby needs to be accepted and not ignored. Those huge eyes, full cheeks and tiny mouth and nose are so appealing and unthreatening that a parent will be sure to give the baby as much attention as possible.

A baby also needs to be stimulated to learn things. Having silky hair and soft skin invites a parent to stroke and groom the baby. In the process, the parent will probably also play with the baby.

A baby needs to be cuddled so that it knows it's safe. Its tiny round body feels wonderfully soft and warm. No wonder a parent delights in holding such a comforting bundle.

But looks aren't everything...

A baby doesn't rely on being cute to make adults want to look after it.
It has other ways to get adults to take care of its needs . . .

Why do babies cry?

I want something! If you've ever heard a baby crying, you know you'll do anything to get it to stop. A baby's cry is pitched at a level that most people can't tolerate for long. And because they find it so stressful to hear, most adults will pick up the crying baby and hold it, feed it, change its diaper or do whatever else it takes to make the baby happy.

If the cry doesn't work, a baby can try another tactic. It will cry and thrash about helplessly. Any adult who takes a look at a baby's tightly screwed-up, grimacing little face and helplessly thrashing arms and legs can't help but want to pick it up.

If a baby is suddenly startled or too roughly handled or played with, it will either cry or try to shut out the source of the alarm by closing its eyes tight, tensing its body and taking deep, ragged breaths. These clues help the baby's parents to know that whatever's happening is more than their baby can handle.

Pick Me Up!

If a baby sees its mother's face it stares intently at her: its eyes widen and its face softens and becomes more alert. The eye contact prompts the mother to stare back, make faces and just generally amuse the little one for as long as it is interested.

This kind of eye-to-eye contact helps to deepen the bond between the two. Sometimes the baby may even crane its neck as it lifts its chin towards her. When the mother sees the baby literally straining to make contact, she will immediately bend down to pick up her baby and cuddle it.

Hold Me More!

A baby even has ways to say it wants to be cuddled some more. If you've held a baby on your shoulder, you'll know that it will automatically turn towards your chest and mold its legs around your side. When the baby gets tired it will put its head against your shoulder and nestle into the crook of your neck. The feeling of the baby's soft little head resting against your neck is irresistible, and you'll cuddle it even more.

Why do my feet get cold so fast?

There's a good reason why your toes are often the first part of you to feel chilly. Heat leaves your body fastest through your toes, fingers, ears and nose. To prevent too much heat loss, your body shuts down the supply of warm blood to these areas as it tries to keep the rest of itself warm and protect sensitive organs. Without an ample supply of warm blood, your toes, fingers, ears and nose soon feel cold. In fact if it gets cold enough they'll even freeze. When that happens you've got frostbite. Ouch!

Why do feet swell up after you've been sitting for a while?

You sit down to watch a movie and slip off your shoes to get really comfortable. But when the movie's over and you try to put your shoes back on, they won't fit. Have they shrunk? No. Your feet have expanded. Because you've been sitting still, much of your body fluid has collected at your lowest point – your feet. When you get up and start walking, you'll get the fluid moving quickly again and soon your feet will shrink back to their normal size.

Why is one foot bigger than the other?

If you're like most people, one big foot isn't your only problem. You might also have mismatched arms, legs or ears. Even at birth nobody's perfect, and we sometimes become more lopsided as we grow because we use one side of our body more than the other and build up bigger muscles. These differences aren't usually a problem, but some unfortunate people have to buy two sizes of shoes to get one pair that fits!

Why do we have toes?

Without toes you probably couldn't stand up. Toes help keep you balanced, and they carry their fair share of your weight too. Your heels support half your weight, your big toes support one-quarter, and your other toes look after the rest. And besides, without toes no one could play "This little piggy went to market"!

Why do feet have arches?

You might think feet could better withstand the pressure of being walked and run on if they were flat instead of arched. But actually the arch is the best shape for supporting weight. Just look at most bridges. To make walking easy, each of your feet has two arches: one that runs from your heel to the ball of your foot to support your weight and one across the ball of your foot to keep you balanced.

Why are feet so ticklish?

If you're like most people, you're probably most ticklish on the soles of your feet. That's because they have a very large concentration of nerve endings, so they're very sensitive. And that's why a tiny stone in your shoe feels like a huge boulder – especially when you walk on it with all your weight.

Why does it hurt so much when you step on something sharp?

Step on a sharp object and bundles of nerves zoom waves of tiny electric shocks from your foot to your spinal column and on to your brain at speeds of 130 m/400 ft per second. So there's not much delay between stepping on the object and feeling the pain. Ouch!

But have you ever noticed how quickly you pull your foot to safety? That's because your spinal column has sent a hasty message to your foot telling it to get off the sharp object — fast! So usually you move your foot away before you've really even felt any pain.

How much electricity does your brain need to work?

Your brain is the most complex computer ever . . . but it operates on only 10 watts of electricity. That's the same amount needed to light up one bulb on a string of outdoor lights!

Can you really have a brainwave?

Even when you're asleep your nerve cells are hard at work. They're passing electric shocks all over your brain to keep you dreaming and breathing, and so on. These messages move like waves, and doctors are able to measure them. When you're sleeping, the waves are large and slow. When you're awake but relaxed, they're faster and smaller. And when you're studying or running fast the waves look sharp and jagged. So if anyone ever tells you that a brilliant idea you've had is a "brainwave," just say you have them all the time!

Can the electricity in your body hurt you?

No. In fact, your body's electricity helps injuries heal faster. When you cut yourself, electricity begins to flow from the cut, creating an electric current. This makes nerves in the injured area grow faster and triggers cells to divide and fill in the cut to start the healing process.

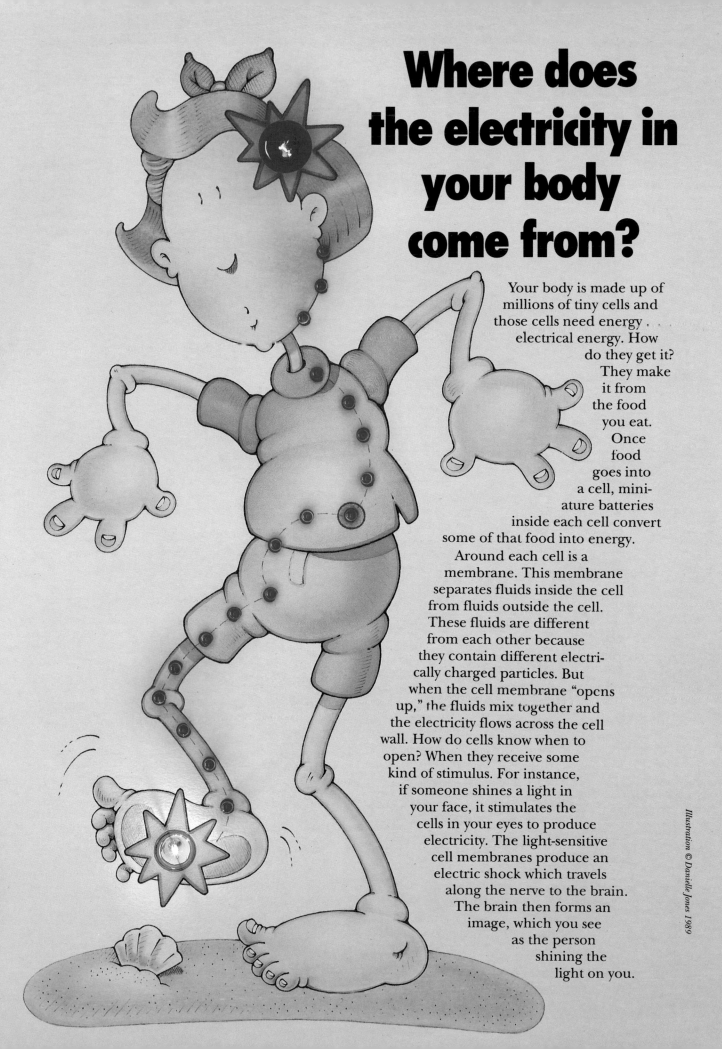

Where does the electricity in your body come from?

Your body is made up of millions of tiny cells and those cells need energy, electrical energy. How do they get it? They make it from the food you eat. Once food goes into a cell, miniature batteries inside each cell convert some of that food into energy. Around each cell is a membrane. This membrane separates fluids inside the cell from fluids outside the cell. These fluids are different from each other because they contain different electrically charged particles. But when the cell membrane "opens up," the fluids mix together and the electricity flows across the cell wall. How do cells know when to open? When they receive some kind of stimulus. For instance, if someone shines a light in your face, it stimulates the cells in your eyes to produce electricity. The light-sensitive cell membranes produce an electric shock which travels along the nerve to the brain. The brain then forms an image, which you see as the person shining the light on you.

Why do my eyelids weigh so much when I'm tired?

Your eyelids don't really get heavier when you're tired, it's just that you lose control over them. When you're asleep, your whole body begins to relax. Instead of being ready for action, your muscles go limp and won't do what you want them to. You're absolutely right when you say "I'm so tired I can't keep my eyes open." And haven't you noticed at about the time your eyelids start to droop how your arms and legs feel oh so heavy, your head nods forward and next thing you know . . .

What happens to my body when I fall asleep?

Sleep is like a mini-holiday for your brain and body: everything relaxes. And because relaxed muscles need less oxygen, your breathing and heart beat slow down. Once this happens, you start to sweat and your body temperature drops slightly. Then about an hour after you fall asleep, your eyeballs start moving rapidly beneath your eyelids as you begin to dream. You drift in and out of dream sleep all night until – rrring! – your alarm clock tells your body the holiday is over.

49

How often do we dream?

People dream four or five times a night, each dream lasting longer than the one before. Most of us spend as much as two hours a night dreaming. To tell if someone's dreaming, watch him closely while he sleeps. If he's lying very still and his eyeballs are moving rapidly beneath his eyelids, he's dreaming. Are his eyes watching what's happening in his dream? No one knows.

What happens to your brain and your body during dreams?

Your brain works by electricity. If this electricity were visible, your brain would appear to be glowing brightly when you are awake. But your sleeping brain would have only an odd spark here and there, except during dreams. Then your brain would glow as if it were awake!

You can toss and turn most of the night, but never while dreaming. That's because your muscles go limp during dreams. Perhaps your brain prevents your muscles from moving so that you don't hurt yourself.

How do scientists learn about dreaming?

Believe it or not, there are places called sleep labs, and people stay overnight there. While they're sleeping, scientists record their brain electricity. It's possible to tell from a brain's electrical activity when a dream starts and ends, but not what the dream was about.

What do animals dream about?

Reptiles and amphibians probably don't dream at all, but it seems that most warm-blooded animals do. All, that is, except for the spiny anteater. Scientists have discovered that this mammal never dreams, but they don't know why.

Cats that have been operated on so that their muscles don't go limp during dreams, have been seen running while asleep, and sometimes even attacking imaginary mice.

Do babies dream?

Newborn babies are great dreamers: they spend about half their sleep time dreaming. Babies even dream before they're born! What do you suppose an unborn baby dreams about?

THE SCI-TECH WORLD

Now it's time to look at the wonders of the world we live in. Speaking of time, did you know that clocks have been around almost as long as people? For thousands of years, people used sundials and other simple clocks to tell time. Then in 1362, scientists built an "astronomical time-telling device," to accurately record the movement of the planets. They discovered that the Earth's movements are regular — it always takes 24 hours for the Earth to spin once on its axis, and about 12 hours to change from day to night. From these discoveries, a clock system was created — one we still use today! Brrring! Brrring! Brrr . . .

If you wake up feeling cold, here's a way to generate heat. Start stretching a thick rubber band. Why does it heat up when you stretch it? If you've ever rubbed your hands together to warm up, you know that friction generates heat. A rubber band is made of millions of long molecules all twisted together. When you stretch it, the molecules rub against each other, creating friction. The more you stretch, the more heat you create and the warmer the rubber band gets. But there's more. The energy you expend stretching the rubber band is transformed into another form of energy, which you feel as heat. So, if you stretch a rubber band again and again, you might end up with something a little to hot to handle!

All this talk of stretching might make you crave a wad of gum. How is bubble gum made? It takes a lot of sugar and corn syrup (to make it sweet), softeners (to give it chewing and blowing action), flavoring (to give it a burst of taste), coloring, gum base (originally from the chicle tree, but now usually synthetic) and glycerin. The ingredients are heated and blended together in a giant mixer. Then the gum's passed between rollers to press it into a long ribbon. Then it's cut up, and stacked to cool. When the gum cools, machines shape it into bubble tape, bubble-gum band-aids, bubble-gum tacos, and plain old gum balls. Be careful when you blow those bubbles — this stuff is sticky!

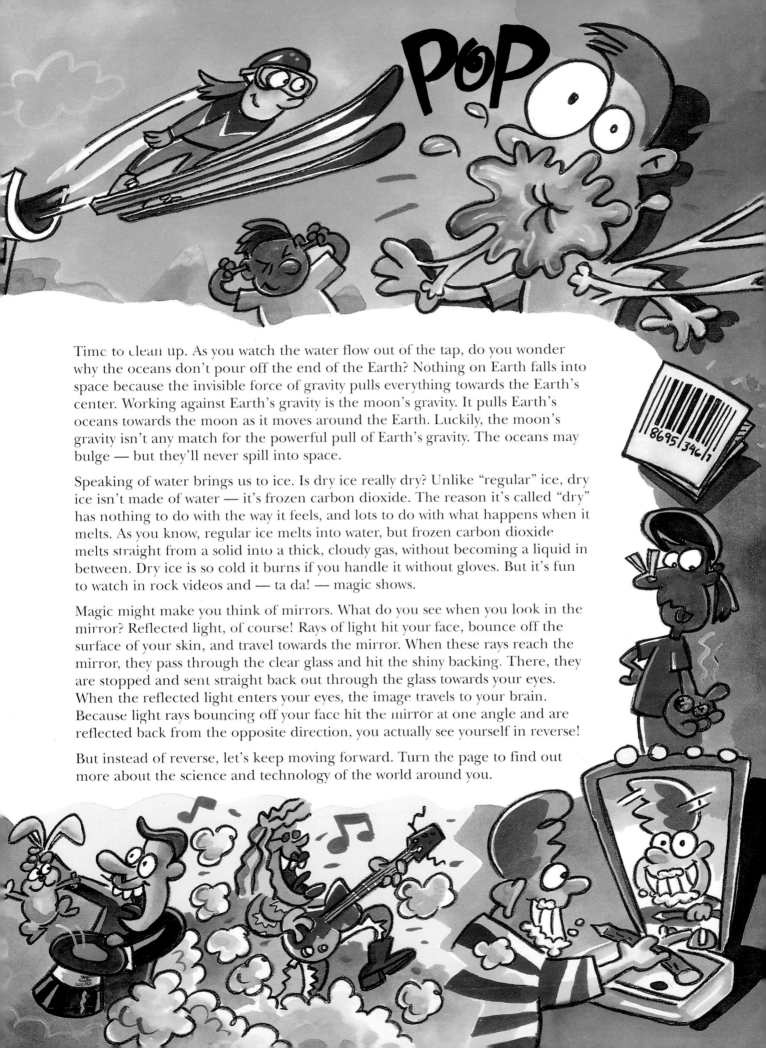

Time to clean up. As you watch the water flow out of the tap, do you wonder why the oceans don't pour off the end of the Earth? Nothing on Earth falls into space because the invisible force of gravity pulls everything towards the Earth's center. Working against Earth's gravity is the moon's gravity. It pulls Earth's oceans towards the moon as it moves around the Earth. Luckily, the moon's gravity isn't any match for the powerful pull of Earth's gravity. The oceans may bulge — but they'll never spill into space.

Speaking of water brings us to ice. Is dry ice really dry? Unlike "regular" ice, dry ice isn't made of water — it's frozen carbon dioxide. The reason it's called "dry" has nothing to do with the way it feels, and lots to do with what happens when it melts. As you know, regular ice melts into water, but frozen carbon dioxide melts straight from a solid into a thick, cloudy gas, without becoming a liquid in between. Dry ice is so cold it burns if you handle it without gloves. But it's fun to watch in rock videos and — ta da! — magic shows.

Magic might make you think of mirrors. What do you see when you look in the mirror? Reflected light, of course! Rays of light hit your face, bounce off the surface of your skin, and travel towards the mirror. When these rays reach the mirror, they pass through the clear glass and hit the shiny backing. There, they are stopped and sent straight back out through the glass towards your eyes. When the reflected light enters your eyes, the image travels to your brain. Because light rays bouncing off your face hit the mirror at one angle and are reflected back from the opposite direction, you actually see yourself in reverse!

But instead of reverse, let's keep moving forward. Turn the page to find out more about the science and technology of the world around you.

Why do racing cyclists bend so low over their handlebars?

How you sit on your bike affects how you battle the force of the wind. On some bikes you sit upright, which is good for comfort. But if you want speed, you have to lower both the handlebars and your shoulders. This makes your chest and shoulders a smaller target area for the wind so it can't push against you as hard and slow you down.

Racers crouch low on their bikes and wear smooth, tight-fitting suits and helmets with a tail so that the air will slide smoothly over them. Racing bikes also have enclosed wheels and frames to further reduce air resistance, adding a tiny bit of extra speed that just might be enough to win.

How do reflectors work?

Believe it or not, the design of the safety reflectors on a bicycle is similar to that of the retroreflectors left on the moon by the Apollo astronauts. Both reflectors contain tiny prisms that bounce light beams back to their source. On Earth, safety reflectors bounce car headlight beams straight back to the driver of the car. On the moon, retroreflectors bounce laser beams back to scientists on Earth. Why? By timing how long the beams take to travel there and back, they can measure the distance between the planet and its moon.

Why does your bicycle have gears?

Gears on your bike allow you to change your rate of pedaling while your wheels maintain their speed going up or down hills. What's the advantage in that? In low gear, your legs move quicker than your wheels, giving you many power strokes in a short distance to help you climb hills or drive through soft sand. High gear gives you many spins of the wheel for only a few strokes of your legs, so you can speed almost effortlessly downhill or along hard, level surfaces. Without gears on your bike, you'd have to pedal at the same speeds that your wheels were turning — wobblingly slow going uphill and furiously fast flying downhill.

● ● ● ● ● ● ● ●

Which are better, fat tires or thin ones?

It depends what you want to do with your bike. Fat tires spread out your weight over a large area. That's why you can ride a mountain bike over sand without sinking in. But as fat, squishy tires roll along, they come in contact with a wide strip of ground, which slows them down. It's known as rolling resistance. Racing tires, on the other hand, are thin and hard, so their contact area with the ground is as small as possible and you have very little resistance to overcome.

Why do you have to lean into a turn when you're biking?

Don't try turning a corner fast without leaning into it — you'll end up on the ground. You must lean into a turn to balance all the forces acting on your bike. At the beginning of the lean, your balancing point, known as your center of mass, is no longer over the wheels, so gravity begins to pull you down. At the same time, centripetal force, produced when your bike begins to turn, forces you towards the inside of the turn. Inertia comes to your rescue, however. This is the tendency of a moving object to keep moving in a straight line, and it's what pulls you towards the outside of the turn and balances the two other forces that pull you in and down.

How ▶ do you make a laser?

LASER is short for "Light Amplification by Stimulated Emission of Radiation." Lasers can be made from gases, liquids or solids, and their power depends on which of these is chosen and how much energy is used to produce them.

A gas laser, for instance, is made by bombarding gas inside a tube with electricity or intense light. This excites the trapped gas, which keeps on building up energy until it must get rid of some of it. As all the tiny, excited bits of gas collide inside the tube, the energy they get rid of creates an incredibly powerful light – laser light.

Will a laser harm you if you get in its way?

Some types of lasers are so powerful they can "zap" you out of your socks.

You certainly wouldn't want to cross the path of the carbon dioxide laser that slices up steel girders or drills holes through diamonds! But low-powered lasers, such as the helium-neon laser that reads the bar codes on your food at check-out counters, won't harm you at all.

Laser light shows are created by argon or krypton gas lasers. When these lasers are shone through glass prisms, they split into the different colors of the rainbow. Though the light from laser shows wouldn't hurt your hand, it could harm your eyes if it shone directly into them. That's why safety barriers are always erected around the laser source at light shows.

Believe it or not, a laser can be focused so precisely that it could be used to put 200 separate holes in the head of a pin!

Why is a laser more powerful than other light beams?

Switch on a flashlight and you'll see that its beam spreads out in a wide V once it leaves the light bulb. But a laser beam doesn't spread out at all. That means that there's no wasted energy, since it's all concentrated in the same direction.

Did You Know That...

• lasers drill holes in baby bottle nipples?
• laser beams carry telephone calls through optical fibers?
• lasers play audio and video discs?
• lasers perform delicate brain, eye and ear surgery?

• industrial lasers weld metals together?
• a laser prints and reads the bar code on your groceries?
• a laser scanner made the color film for this book?

Why do you sink in quicksand?

On the surface quicksand looks like solid ground. But it's really a pit filled with water and loose wet sand. If you weigh more than an ant and you step on quicksand, you'll sink because the water can't support your weight. The deeper you sink, the more sand there is in the water to weigh you down. If you get caught in quicksand, don't panic. Lie flat on your back and spread out your arms and legs. You'll float to safety.

On a hot day, why does a long asphalt road look like it has water on it?

You might find it hard to believe, but that puddle of water down the road is really a reflection of the sky. What is it reflected by? The road? No, by a "mirror" formed by bent rays of light. Light waves travel faster through cooler air. When light rays from the sky reach the hot air rising off a hot black road, they bend. At the point where they bend, the light rays act like a mirror reflecting an image of the sky. The image is known as a mirage. And sometimes, a mirage can be upside down. For example, at sea the layers of air near the water can focus light waves from a ship into an upside-down image in the sky. So if you see an upside-down ship on the horizon, don't call the coast guard. It's merely a mirage.

SANBORN

Why do you have to punch two holes in a large juice can to let the juice out?

It has to do with vacuums — spaces without gases, liquids or solids. When juice leaves the can, air rushes in to replace it or else a vacuum forms where the juice used to be. When you pour from a can with just one hole in it, you get a squirt of juice and then nothing but a "glug glug" sound as air is sucked in through the hole. You have to wait until the space left by the squirting juice fills with air before you get more juice. But if you punch two holes in the can, air goes in one hole as juice flows freely out the other one.

What's a googol?

A dripping faucet? A big number? A large gull-like bird? If you chose "a big number," you're right! A googol is a big number and we're not talking about a mere 1,000,000. A googol is a number written as "1" followed by 100 zeros. And if a googol is not a big enough number, there's a googol-plex as well. That's a googol times a googol. Mind-boogling!

Who first used umbrellas?

Only extremely important people were allowed to use umbrellas or parasols in ancient China, India, Persia and Africa. The King of Burma called himself The Lord of the Great Parasol. These early umbrellas were colorful, large and impressive; a crowd could easily pick out the important person with an umbrella when nobody else had one. One of the first umbrellas in Europe was brought there from Persia by Jonas Hanway in 1750. People who saw him walking with it thought he was quite mad.

Why are storm clouds gray, while other clouds are white?

Lie outside on your back on a sunny day and watch the clouds go by. Notice many all-white clouds? Probably not – even fine-weather clouds have some gray parts. That's because some part of each cloud is in shadow – and it's the shadows that cause the gray. The gray color is also caused by water droplets in the cloud – the bigger the drops, the darker the cloud. On stormy days there are lots of water droplet-filled clouds around casting shadows. When you see them, get out your umbrella.

How much snow would have to fall to give an inch of rain?

You'd need a pretty big snowfall to make the equivalent of an inch of rain. The ratio is 10 to 1. That means ten inches of snow melted down would give you one inch of rain. And imagine this: In one cup of snow you'll find more than 10 million snowflakes! Better get out your shovel.

What does "It smells like rain" mean?

Almost everything smells stronger before it rains. Why? It has to do with the force of air pressing down on you. During fine weather the air pressure is high, but it drops before a storm. This lower pressure allows odors to escape into the air more freely than usual. So it's not the rain you're smelling – you're smelling more of everything.

Why do ski jumpers almost touch their noses to their skis when they're soaring through the air?

Leaning forward at that uncomfortable-looking angle helps a skier jump farther. Air flows faster over the curve of his back than below him, and faster-moving air means less air pressure. That creates lift, which helps the jumper stay in the air longer and so travel farther.

How do skiers know which wax to put on their skis?

Before skiers can put wax on their skis they must first check the temperature and snow conditions to know which wax to apply. Here's why they need to know. All snowflakes have six pointed arms. But old snowflakes, or "warm" snowflakes, have lost the points on their arms. For a skier to get a grip on this kind of slippery snow, she needs to use a soft wax so that the snowflake's shortened arms can poke into it and take hold. New or "cold" snowflakes have longer, sharper arms, so they stick to wax a lot more easily. Using a hard wax ensures that this dry snow won't stick to the skis too much and slow the skier down.

Why do downhill racers use oddly bent poles?

It has to do with streamlining. The curve in those poles allows them to wrap closely around the skier's waist to reduce the slowing effect of the air he has to race through. And the special covers on the baskets at the ends of the poles direct the air around him and steady him. The skier further streamlines himself by zooming down the hill with his back almost parallel to his skis, elbows tucked inside his knees, head pulled in and hands near his chin. It's fondly known as the "egg position."

How is it possible to skip a flat rock over water?

It all has to do with bouncing bellyflops. When you bellyflop, you hit the water with your flat front. Ouch! It hurts because for a split second the water resists moving out of your way. You sink immediately, of course, because you're heavy and were travelling downward to begin with. But a flat rock, moving at high speed across the water, does a bouncing bellyflop. Because it only touches the surface for a fraction of a second, the water doesn't have time to get out of the way and let the rock sink. Eventually, the rock slows down, gravity takes over and . . . plop. Time to look for a new rock.

Why can't you see your reflection in rough water?

Look down into choppy water and there's no reflection, right? Wrong. You might not believe this but even when water is rough it's still reflecting. Instead of one smooth surface that looks and acts like a large mirror, however, the waves in rough water make lots of small surfaces that reflect in many different directions. So you get lots of tiny reflections that are so scattered you can't possibly see them all. This doesn't just apply to water. Any surface will reflect, but if it's not smooth the reflection is broken up and unclear.

What makes ice cubes crack when you put them in a drink?

No matter how cold your drink is, it's still warmer than a frozen ice cube. So when you plop in an ice cube, the drink warms up the outside of the cube. Meanwhile, the inside of the cube stays just as cold as it ever was. Alas, a warm outside that's trying to expand and a cold inside that wants to stay the same means trouble. Eventually the stress becomes too great and – crrrack! Ice cube breakdown.

Why does ice some-times stick to your fingers?

When you pick up an ice cube, heat from your fingers melts a thin layer of ice. If the ice cube is very cold, this layer of moisture quickly refreezes, sticking your fingers to the cube. Most small freezers in the top of refrigerators don't chill ice cold enough to do this, but some freezers can. When metal freezes, the same thing can occur. That's why you need to be careful not to touch frozen metal with your bare hands or tongue.

Why does a newspaper tear smoothly up and down but not from side to side?

Take a close look at a piece of newspaper through a magnifying glass and you'll see that it's made up of tiny wood fibers. If your glass is powerful enough, you'll see that the fibers all line up in the same direction, up and down on the page. This gives the sheet of newspaper a grain, something like the grain in meat. When you tear the newspaper from top to bottom it tears evenly because you're tearing in the direction of the grain. But when you tear it from side to side, it tears unevenly because you're tearing across the grain.

Why do clocks run clockwise?

Mechanical clocks were created in the northern hemisphere by inventors trying to make models of the sun's movement in the sky.

To watch the sun from the northern hemisphere, you have to face south. Then the sun will rise on your left and pass over your head to set on your right. Since the hour hand on a clock was made to follow the sun's motion through the sky, it moves from left to right over the top of the clock —

clockwise. Just think . . . if clocks had been invented in the southern hemisphere, they might run in the opposite direction.

Why do boats have round windows instead of square ones?

When windows were first put in boats about 300 years ago, their frames were cast in bronze and iron. It was easier to spin the metal into a smooth, circular shape on a lathe than to mold it into a square. Also, round port-holes — or as sailors call them, portlights — were easier to open and close and could be made watertight. Today, thanks to better metal-working techniques, square portlights are becoming fashionable because they let in more light. Unfortunately, some of them also let in water at the corners.

Why does thick syrup pile up when it's poured?

When you pour milk over shredded wheat, it flows evenly over the cereal. But when you pour thick syrup onto pancakes, the syrup piles up on itself. Why? Syrup's thick, sticky consistency causes it to hold together. So when it's poured, the bottom part of the drip touches the surface of the syrup but doesn't disappear into the body of the syrup. Instead it folds over, piling up into little mounds. But after a moment those little mounds flatten out and the thick, sticky syrup cascades down the sides of your pancakes. Yum.

Does all milk taste the same?

Not every milk-producing animal says "Moo!" Milk can come from water buffalo, goats, reindeer or horses and each milk tastes a little different. All milk is made up of milk fat, lactose (milk sugar), protein, minerals and water, but the amounts of each ingredient vary in each animal's milk. Horse's milk is high in water and lactose but low in fat, so it's watery and sweet. Reindeer's milk is high in fat, low in water, with only a little lactose, so it's thick and creamy. Even cow's milk can taste different. In some places milk is pasteurized (heated to kill bacteria) or homogenized (processed so the milk fat doesn't float to the top). And it's available with different amounts of milk fat left in or skimmed off. So if you drink lots of milk, you just may notice a dairy difference!

Why do most cereals crackle when you add milk to them?

When milk sits in a carton in the fridge, it's perfectly quiet. And when puffed rice cereal sits in its box, it doesn't crackle or pop. So why all the noise when you mix the two together? It has to do with the way the cereal is made. Puffed rice cereal is made by heating the ingredients at very high temperatures. When that happens, water inside each bit of rice expands suddenly and blows it up like a balloon, leaving each piece with very tiny cavities all over its surface. (If you look closely at your cereal, or put a piece under a magnifying glass, you'll see these tiny holes.) When milk is added, it flows over these little cavities and traps air inside them. Then, as the milk slowly starts to seep into the tiny holes, it forces the air out. And it's that air being released that you hear as a "pop" or a "crackle."

What makes popcorn ◀ pop?

Inside every popcorn kernel is a drop or two of water. When you cook corn in very hot oil, the water inside the kernels heats up and begins to turn to steam. As you continue cooking the corn, more and more water becomes steam. Fortunately for popcorn-lovers, steam takes up more room than water. So when the steam pressure inside the kernels finally becomes too much for their walls, the popcorn kernels explode — snap, crackle, boom!

How do rubber bands stretch?

If you've ever stretched out a Slinky toy, then let it coil up again, you've seen more or less what happens to the molecules inside a rubber band. Rubber molecules are hooked together so they can stretch into long chains when pulled, then coil up again when the pressure's removed.

Why does a compass always point north?

Did you know that you're whirling through space on a magnet? Yes, the earth is a powerful magnet. A compass needle is also a magnet, though a very tiny one. The north-seeking pole of the compass needle can't help but be attracted to the north pole of the earth.

Why do pennies stink after being in your hand?

Hold a penny tightly in your hand for a few minutes, then sniff it. Yuck! What a stink! There are two things that make that smell – the copper in the penny and your sweat. Copper is a very absorbent metal and it easily picks up sulphur from the air. This not only makes the penny dirty; it also combines with the acids in your perspiration to make hydrogen sulphide. That's the stuff that smells like rotten eggs. The more sulphur and sweat the penny reacts with, the smellier it gets. But remember, it's not worth more just because it's got an extra scent. (Groan!)

Why can't I blow bubbles with regular gum?

All gums contain the same ingredients: flavoring, sweeteners, gum base and wood resin. Yum yum. The flavoring and sweeteners are what make you loyal to your favorite brand, and the gum base is a kind of rubber that keeps your gum from breaking down as you chew it. It's the wood resin, a sticky, elastic substance, that makes chewing gum stretchy. To turn chewing gum into bubble gum, all you need to do is stir in more wood resin. Then when you blow a bubble, the extra wood resin allows the bubble's thin film to keep stretching while you blow and blow until ...POP! Ooops, better wipe the gum off your face and start again! Even resin has a breaking point.

Why do table knives have round ends?

The knife was one of our earliest inventions, used for fighting, hunting, carving and, of course, for cutting food. The problem of people fighting with knives at mealtimes brought about the invention of table manners. In 1699, the king of France ruled that table knives should have round ends to stop dinner guests from sticking knives into each other or picking their teeth with the cutlery. Table knives have had round ends ever since.

Who first used forks?

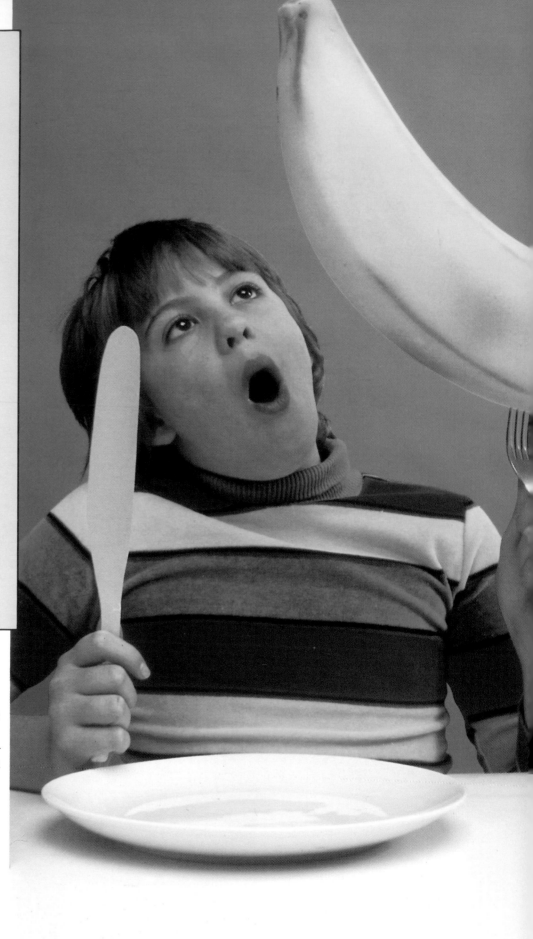

Rich people were the first to use forks, to keep their lace-ruffled sleeves out of the gravy. As the custom spread, the way food was served changed too. Instead of everyone taking food from a shared dish, each diner got an individual helping. The invention of the fork also ended the need for washing our hands during dinner: a table napkin is all we need.

Why do refrigerators turn bananas black?

Bananas are a tropical fruit. That means they grow best in warm countries where the days are sunny and hot and the nights don't get too cold. Bananas can't withstand cold temperatures. When you put a banana in the fridge, it reacts to the cold temperature just as it would react to being frozen on the plant. It produces compounds — called polyphenals — that turn the fruit black. First the skin turns black. Then, if you wait long enough, the fruit inside will turn black too.

Why do bananas get bruised as they age?

Bananas turn black as they get older even if they have never been touched, so those black spots aren't bruises. They're caused by a hormone called ethylene that helps fruit ripen. Unfortunately, ethylene doesn't know when to stop ripening, and eventually it turns the banana black. There's no way to prevent the production of ethylene, although you can slow it down by storing your bananas in a cool place. But keep them out of the refrigerator, or you'll have the blackest bananas on the block before you can say "peanut butter and banana sandwich."

Why don't bananas have seeds?

And what have bananas got to do with the high-tech world? Unzip a banana and take a look inside. Lots of pulp and no seeds means that the banana doesn't grow naturally in the wild — it's an "invention" of ours. Thousands of years ago, wild bananas were like big bean pods filled with seeds. Using science to improve their lives — and their diets — Southeast Asians learned to breed pulpy, seedless bananas. Some bananas are not sweet, but are picked green and boiled, fried, broiled, dried, made into beer or turned into soup. Only sweet bananas are eaten raw. In North America, more sweet bananas are eaten every day than any other fruit.

Why does gum go hard after you've chewed it?

Ever run your hand under a chair you're sitting on and suddenly felt a disgusting glob of someone else's old gum? It's revolting — and it's hard as a rock because the ingredients that made it soft are long gone. Softeners keep gum pliable by helping it hold in moisture. But as you chew the gum, you also chew the softeners out of it. When you finally take it out of your mouth, all the moisture evaporates because there aren't any softeners left to hold on to the moisture.

Why do drinking glasses slide across the counter when they're wet?

When you place a wet glass rim-side down, hot water runs down its inside and outside surfaces onto the counter. The water in the glass evaporates, changing from a liquid to a gas. Gas molecules take up more room than liquid molecules, so the air pressure increases inside the glass. If the glass isn't too heavy, the gas molecules lift it as they try to escape to the lower air pressure outside. You can see bubbles of escaping air at the glass's rim. Not only does the hot water help lift the glass, it also makes the counter slippery — and zoom! Off goes your glass.

Zooommmm

Why does grease run away from soap?

Next time you're washing dishes, take the greasiest pan you can find and fill it with clear warm water. See the blobs of grease floating on the water's surface instead of sinking and mixing with the water? They can't mix with the water because water molecules cling so tightly to each other that they form a surface "skin," keeping other molecules out. Now drop some detergent on the water in the center of the pan and watch those oily blobs zip away from it. Detergent is specially made to link up molecules of water with molecules of oil. This reduces the clinging power of water molecules so much that the water's "skin" gets a hole in it. The torn "skin" shrinks out to the edge of the pan, carrying the oil with it.

What is a sponge?

A sponge is a very simple animal — it doesn't have a head, a mouth, arms, or legs. Instead it's made up of tiny, microscopic cells that grow very close together. Most sponges live in shallow seas around the world, although a few live in fresh water. Some live alone, others live together in colonies. Some sponges are so small you can barcly scc thcm. Some can be larger than a bathtub and others can be up to 2 m/6 ½ ft tall. Some are dull orange or brown, others are bright red or green. Each kind of cell in a sponge has a different job. Some form the skeleton of the sponge and give it its shape, while others serve as protective cells. Some cells stir up the water to make it flow through the sponge, others have holes to allow the water to filter through. Some take in food particles from the water as it flows through, others pass the food to inner cells. And some cells are just for reproduction.

Although most dishwashing sponges are man-made, bath sponges are usually the skeleton of an animal that once lived off the coast of Florida or Greece. Once collected, the sponges are left to dry in the sun so that the soft tissues rot. Then they are pounded and washed, leaving only what's called the spongin skeleton. This skeleton is made up of a network of elastic fibers that can absorb and hold water, and can be squeezed too.

Sponges that don't end up in your bathroom may be eaten by sea slugs, sea stars, turtles and some tropical fishes.

Illustration © Danielle Jones 1989

Why can't I float in my bathtub? ▶

Dive into a pool and you soon bob up to the surface. But climb into a bathtub and you remain sitting on the bottom. Why do you float in a big pool and sink in a small tub? The size of the container and the amount of water in it makes the difference. To float, there must be enough water for you to sink down to the point of "equilibrium." What's equilibrium? It's the point at which your body pushes out of the way an amount of water that weighs the same as you – the rest of the liquid, which had been holding up that water, holds you up instead. In a big pool there's room for you to push the water out of the way and still have plenty of water left between you and the bottom of the pool. Because your weight equals the weight of the water you've moved, you float. But in a bathtub, unless it happens to be huge and you're very small, you weigh more than the water you're able to move, so you sink.

How did people figure out soap would get you clean?

Until about 2,000 years ago people in Europe washed by coating themselves with mud, then scraping it off with an iron instrument. To soothe their sore skin, they rubbed oil all over themselves. In those days, oily skin was considered beautiful. It was the Gauls from Southern France who invented soap. They used to plaster their hair with goat fat and ash to make it fashionably stiff. They then discovered that when they mixed their hair "gel" with water, it cleaned dirt and grease off their skin. Now oily skin isn't too trendy – except at the beach.

What are bathtubs made of?

The first modern bathtubs were wooden. Some were plated with metal, but they were scratchy and leaked. Rich people bought smooth china bathtubs, but they were so cold you had to put pillows inside to sit on. Then all-metal baths arrived – they were smooth and warmed up quickly. These tubs were covered in paint to keep them from rusting. But the paint sometimes dissolved in hot water, turning the unlucky bather a peculiar color. Finally, someone decided to cover a metal tub in hard enamel. At last, a truly comfortable bath. The quest for the best bathtub continues, however. The latest tubs are made of acrylic. Their main advantage? They aren't cold when you lean back for a soak and a good read.

How did people clean their teeth before toothbrushes were invented?

The first toothbrush was a good-tasting twig, chewed until one end shredded and could be used as a brush.

In many places people still chew a stick a day. Later, hardy types cleaned their teeth with a finger dipped in salt or chalk. Toothpicks were popular – the rich wore jeweled picks on chains or stuck them in their hats. Toothbrushes with gold and silver handles and hog bristles arrived 300 years ago. Wooden ones cheap enough for most people to buy arrived 200 years later. And the rest is history.

How much water do you use in a day?

f you're like the average North American, you use about 325 L/71 gal – more than two bathtubs full. But what do you do with all that water? For instance, how much water do you flush down the toilet every day?

Check out these figures: flushing the toilet uses up 110 L/22 gal, watering the garden, washing the car, 90 L/20 gal, drinking and cooking, 11 L/2 gal, washing clothes, dishes and self, 124 L/27 gal.

(P.S. If you gave up having baths, washing dishes and doing laundry, you could cut your family's water bill by almost a third.)

How come neon light is so bright?

Neon lights are long glass tubes filled with neon gas — a substance made up of neon atoms. Tiny electrons move around each atom in circles called orbits. When a neon light is turned on, electricity flows from one end of the tube to the other. The electrical charge "excites" the electrons and makes them jump out of their orbit, leaving behind an empty space. The space is immediately filled by another excited electron from another atom. As this electron settles into its spot, it releases its energy, which is seen as a bright glow.

Why doesn't a car radio work under a bridge?

"**A**nd the cat burglar is . . . ." Oh no! Now you'll never know! You drove under a bridge and lost the radio signal on the AM band. That's because the sound travels through the air to your car radio in invisible "waves." The waves pass easily between air molecules, which are flexible and move around. But the molecules in metal and concrete bridges are bonded together so tightly they block sound waves. The waves can't reach the antenna — and you're left without a sound.

Why do you hear a "bang" when a balloon breaks?

The sound you hear is an explosion of air. When you blow up a balloon, you force millions of air molecules into a small space. You can't see them, but they stretch the balloon every time you blow. When the balloon breaks, these molecules burst out and bump the air molecules in the room. A chain reaction of this bumping travels toward your ears and enters your eardrums a split-second later, causing strong vibrations. You hear these vibrations as a "bang" — a sound that warns you and others to avoid getting too close.

How do fireworks work? ▲

Fireworks are made up of gunpowder and various chemicals. These are all packed into a laminated paper tube along with a small fuse.

Getting a firecracker to burn is a two-stage process. When the fuse is lit the gunpowder explodes, launching the firecracker into the air like a rocket. Once the firecracker is airborne, the fuse ignites the rest of the ingredients. The colors you see showering the sky depend upon the chemicals and metals in the firecracker. Different chemicals burn in different colors. Strontium and lithium compounds, for example, burn red, barium ones burn green, copper salts and compounds burn blue, and sodium ones burn yellow. Carbon and metallic lead, iron and aluminum create sparks, and charcoal is sometimes used to create the brightly colored "tails" that streak across the dark night sky.

All these chemicals mean that fireworks displays are very dangerous. So make sure you get an expert to set off your next show.

How can you make glow-in-the-dark stuff?

Take a few Wintergreen Life Savers and a mirror into a *very* dark closet. Pop two candies into your mouth and, watching your open mouth in the mirror, crunch down on them. If you crunch hard enough you should see a green flash. Why? Scientists think they've finally found the answer for this phenomenon, which is called "triboluminescence." They've discovered that the flashes come from the way the crystals in certain materials are put together. The crystals of triboluminescent material are arranged irregularly. So when these crystals break apart, positive and negative electrical charges in the crystals separate, leaving holes between them. The charges then leap across these spaces to recombine. These "leaps" stir up nitrogen molecules in the air and produce a blue-green glow, which is the flash you see.

Why do some Frisbees glow in the dark?

There's nothing quite as magic as a yo-yo or a Frisbee glowing in the dark. How do they do it? They glow because they're made of special phosphorescent compounds.

Any object absorbs energy when light is shone on it. The light "excites" the molecules within the object, making them highly energized.

However, these molecules would prefer to return to the calm, relaxed state they were in before the light started shining. To release their excess energy and get back to normal, they radiate the energy in the form of light and heat. Usually the light is radiated much too quickly for the human eye to see. But with some special compounds, such as calcium sulphide, the light trickles out over seconds or hours. And it's that stored-up light you see glowing in the dark as it's released.

OUT OF THIS WORLD

Next step out takes us to the mysteries of space. Did you know that *all* the stars you see in the night sky are part of a huge, wheel-shaped system called the Milky Way Galaxy? Our sun is just one of billions of stars in the Milky Way. The center of the Milky Way is about 24,000 light-years away from Earth. And how far is that? One light-year is the distance light travels in a year, about 10 trillion km (6 trillion miles). A trillion is a one followed by 12 zeroes. So that makes the center of the Milky Way an astronomical 240,000,000,000,000,000 km (144,000,000,000,000,000 miles) away! Want to see the center of the Milky Way? Face south during an evening in August to October and look above the horizon.

At the same time, you might see an enormous moon looming on the horizon. It's called a harvest moon, since it's often seen in late summer and early fall. Why is it so big? Try this simple experiment. One night, when the moon is high, hold a ruler at arm's length and measure the moon. Then, on another night, measure the moon when it's low on the horizon. You may be surprised to find that both measurements are the same. The size difference you thought you'd find is just an optical illusion — your brain fooled you, although nobody knows exactly why. It's probably that when the moon is overhead, there's nothing familiar nearby to compare it to, and so it looks small. When it's low in the sky, it looks big compared to the tiny trees, buildings or hills on the horizon.

All this looking into the distance makes you want to just take off, doesn't it? How long would it take to walk to Mars? Haul on your springiest shoes and get set for a very long stroll. If you left Earth today and walked at an ordinary walking speed for 12 hours each day, you wouldn't reach Mars for almost 2500 years! That's a long walk, especially since you'd have to hold your breath the whole time in the vacuum of space.

Speaking of vacuums, have you ever wondered where something goes if it gets sucked into a black hole in space? Black holes are very weird things. Yet astronomers are almost certain they really exist. They think that when a giant star explodes, its core bursts inwards with tremendous force, crushing the star out of existence. Now here's the weird part of the theory. All that's left after the implosion is the star's gravitational field, or what's known as a black hole. If something gets near a black hole, it can't escape the huge amount of gravity and gets sucked in. First it gets stretched like a piece of spaghetti. Then, each atom in it is crushed out of existence. But don't worry — as long as you stay on Earth, there's no chance at all of falling into a black hole. And why are black holes black? It's because not even light can escape the gravitational field.

Did you know that moonlight is not really produced by the moon itself? Instead, the moon reflects the light of the sun. The moon is often still in the sky during the day, but you don't usually notice it because the sun is so much brighter. Night or day, the moon moves around the Earth, so you won't always be able to see it even if you look for it. At the dark of the moon, you can't see the moon at all. And when the moon is full, you'll see all of its face at night, but don't crane your neck trying to see it during the day . That's when the moon is on the other side of the Earth. About a week after a full moon, the moon is in the right place in the sky to reflect the sun's light and be seen during early morning. If you look in the eastern sky before breakfast, you'll probably see it. What a way to start your day — with sunlight and moonlight.

Turn the page to shed a little light on other out-of-this-world wonders.

▲ Why doesn't Earth have a ring around it?

Scientists think that the planets that have rings hold the clue to tell us why Earth *doesn't* have one. The ringed planets, Saturn, Jupiter, Uranus and most probably Neptune, are all giant gas planets, many times bigger and with stronger gravitational forces than Earth. It's easy for them to attract and hold on to chunks of ice, rocks, dust or frozen gas that make up their ring systems. They all have several small moons, which might also help to keep the rings in place. As well, all the gas planets are a great distance from the sun, so their rings aren't exposed to much damage from the powerful solar wind. Compared to these great ringed giants, tiny Earth with its weak gravity, single large moon and closeness to the sun probably never stood much of a chance of holding on to a ring for very long – if at all.

If the earth is moving around the sun, why can't we feel it?

Not only is the earth spinning like a top but it's also moving through space at 250 km/s/155 miles per second. That's a breathtaking speed, so why can't you feel any of this movement? Being on the earth is like being in a smooth elevator. The only way you know it's moving is if it slows down or speeds up. Since the earth travels smoothly at the same speed all the time, there are no changes to let you know you're moving.

Why is the sun yellow?

Next time you barbecue hamburgers, watch the charcoal embers as they cool. They'll turn from white to orange to red. It's the same with stars. The hottest ones burn blue, the coolest red. In between are white, yellow and orange stars. Fortunately for us, our sun is a stable, medium-temperature, yellow star. In late fall, winter and early spring you can see another bright yellow star. During those times look overhead in the dark night sky for Capella, in the constellation Auriga.

Which is colder, the North or South Pole?

Brrrr. In August 1960 the temperature near the South Pole dropped to a record-breaking -88.3°C/-127°F. The South Pole is usually colder than the North. Why? It's on solid ground, high up on a mountain, where the temperature is colder than at sea level. The North Pole, of course, sits on an ice cap over the Arctic Ocean. You might not think the Arctic Ocean is too warm, but it's warm enough to raise the temperature around the North Pole by a few degrees.

What's the "Great Red Spot" on Jupiter?

In March 1979, the robot spacecrafts Voyager I and II began to send back to Earth pictures of Jupiter. These photographs revealed that one of the planet's biggest mysteries, the Great Red Spot, is a swirling hurricane three times larger than Earth. Some years the spot is bright red, and other years it's salmon colored. Scientists think the color change could be due to different amounts of red phosphorus.

Voyager also confirmed that Jupiter is a world of whirling clouds and poisonous gases. Great lightning storms rage around the planet and winds of up to 400 km/h /250 mph whip the clouds across the sky. Jupiter's very faint ring may have been created when a moon got too close and broke into small pieces.

Why is space so cold?

The space in between all those far-flung stars is mostly a big stretch of nothing, an airless vacuum. This means that there's not much dust or gas in space that could trap and hold the heat from all those stars. So the heat, in the form of radiation, simply keeps on traveling. Eventually the radiation strikes something big enough to absorb its heat, for instance planets and moons, but the space in between them never heats up. No one knows for sure, but scientists guess that the temperature in space could be as low as -273°C/ -459°F. Scientists call this absolute zero. It's certainly absolutely cold!

Why doesn't air leak into space?

Relax! Before anything can escape the tremendous pull of Earth's gravity, it must achieve a speed of 11 km/s or 7 miles per second! That's how fast the space shuttle leaves Earth, and that's the speed our air must achieve before it can escape into space. And that's not likely to happen. A hurricane blows only about 120 km/h/75 mph.

Can a jet fly into outer space?

What's to stop the fastest jet on Earth from flying up to the moon? Many things, just one being that as soon as the plane left Earth's atmosphere (assuming it could fly fast enough to escape Earth's gravity) its jet engines would die. That's because jet engines need oxygen to operate, and there isn't any oxygen in space. Without engine power, the plane would eventually be pulled back to Earth.

Why are there still footprints on the moon?

On July 20, 1969, millions of television viewers around the world watched spellbound as U.S. astronaut Neil Armstrong climbed down from the lunar module Eagle onto the dusty surface of the moon. Soon he was joined by Edwin (Buzz) Aldrin, Jr., and together they spent the next 21½ hours setting up experiments and bounding around like kangaroos in the weak lunar gravity. All those footprints they left — and those of later Apollo astronauts — are still there today, looking exactly as they did when they were first made. Why? The moon has no atmosphere so there is no wind or weather to blow or wash away the imprints of the first pairs of authentic moon boots. Tiny meteorites that constantly fall on the moon will eventually erode the footprints, but that will take millions of years.

Why is the moon round?

If you think the moon is round, guess again. It's egg-shaped, and the pointed end, which has the thinner crust, always faces the earth.

Some scientists think that the earth's strong gravitational pull may have sucked the moon into this shape.

Where did the moon come from?

Even though the moon is Earth's nearest neighbor in space, astronomers still aren't sure how it formed. The best theory is that another planet about the size of Mars smashed into Earth just after it formed. When the crash happened, a huge amount of rock was blasted off into the space around Earth. Later, this material collected into a body one-quarter the size of the earth's diameter – and became known as the moon.

Could a balloon float up to the moon?

Think of how much money NASA would save if astronauts could travel to the moon by balloon! Alas, it will never happen. To rise, balloons must be filled with a gas that's lighter than air. But if they rise high enough above the earth, the air they're floating through becomes as thin and "light" as the gas inside the balloon. And once the balloon isn't lighter than the air, it will stop rising. Scientists think a balloon could rise about 30 km/20 miles before it stopped dead. So much for ballooning to the moon.

Is there ever a blue moon?

Once in a blue moon, the moon really does appear to turn blue. The last time a blue moon was seen was in 1950. Scientists believe it was caused when a thicker than usual blanket of dust filtered out red light in the earth's atmosphere, leaving the moon looking decidedly blue.

Can you ever see the other side of the moon?

You won't ever see this view of the moon from your bedroom window. It's the far side of the moon and it's never visible from Earth. The moon is locked so tightly into its orbit by the earth's strong gravitational pull that it can't turn fast enough to show us its other side.

What are the Northern Lights?

The Northern Lights are ribbons of red, pink, and ghostly green light that dance and shimmer for hours across the sky. They occur when the sun bombards Earth with tiny particles of electricity, too small for us to see. When these particles hit the highest part of Earth's atmosphere, they electrify the air and make it glow.

Why are the Northern Lights different colors? Each gas in Earth's atmosphere glows with its own color when it becomes charged with electricity. Oxygen gives off an eerie green glow, nitrogen glows red and neon gas turns pink.

Why is a black hole black?

A black hole has such strong gravity that not even a single ray of light can escape. And that means that the black hole can't be seen against the blackness of space. So how do scientists know a black hole is there, you ask? By watching the behavior of stars nearby. Here's how.

If a black hole is in close orbit around a star, gases coming off the star are sucked into the black hole by its gravity. As the gases get pulled in, they get squeezed and heated. When this happens energy is released in the form of gamma rays and X-rays. These rays, which can be detected by scientists on Earth, tell that a black hole is orbiting nearby. Eventually the star will be swallowed up by the black hole.

Why is the moon light and dark when you look at it?

When you look up at the moon parts of it are bright and clear and other parts are shady and dark. Those dark and light markings are caused by mountains and "scas." The seas are not made of water. They're big flat areas of lava that flowed and solidified long ago. Since the lava material is darker than the material that makes up the mountains, the rough mountain areas look light and the large, flat lava plains look dark.

What does it sound like in space?

Sound travels through the air as vibrations. When the vibrating air touches your ear drum and sets it vibrating, you hear the sound. There is no air in space for sound waves to travel on, so space is totally silent.

Why does Earth look blue from outer space?

Earth looks blue from outer space because so much of it is covered with water.

Could people live on Uranus?

Uranus, a massive blue-green ice planet, is a dark mysterious world wrapped in an atmosphere of poisonous methane. At its center is thought to be a rocky core about the size of our planet, surrounded by a slushy methane ocean 20,000 km/ 12,500 mi deep. Needless to say, it's not a world where humans could live.

How do space probes know where they're going?

A space probe is a robot, plain and simple. Actually, it's a robot, fancy and complicated. Its computer "brain" is bursting with information about where it's going, how to get there, and everything else from "blast-off" to "mission accomplished." It can also collect data about the planets, moons and other "sign posts" it passes while in space.

All of this information helps a probe stay on course and out of trouble. But if it needs a long-distance hand, the scientists back home send radio signals that tell the probe how to use its rocket motors to adjust course. A probe may be an out-of-this-world robot, but without the brainiacs back on Earth, it could become a lost cause.

What's so hot about the Hubble?

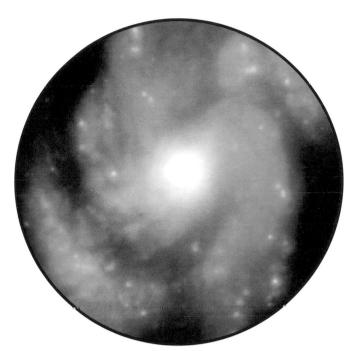

Everyone thought the Hubble Space Telescope would be the greatest telescope in the world. But they didn't count on Hubble-troubles like blurry vision and shaky solar panels. They didn't figure that by the time the Hubble was in orbit and over its problems, there would be ground-based telescopes big enough to see just as far as the Hubble could. So then, what's so hot about the Hubble? Even the best ground-based telescopes can't detect some things — like objects in ultraviolet light blocked by Earth's atmosphere — that the Hubble can. And even if they can see as far as the Hubble does, they can't produce separate, clear images of objects that are very close together. The Hubble can. Which means that the Hubble not only can see to the edge of the universe, but can also clearly show us what's there.

Before Hubble's troubles were fixed, things looked blurry. After, its sight improved. Things now look clearer (below).

Do space probes ever meet aliens?

So far none have — but Voyager probes are ready to do so! Voyagers travelling through space each carry a gold-plated, audio-visual disc just in case the spacecraft is found by intelligent aliens. The disc contains images of our planet and its life forms, scientific information, and sounds of Earth, including whales singing, a baby crying, waves breaking on a shore, and music.

Who got to name the planets?

What did eleven-year-old Venetia Burney (who was born in 1919) have in common with astronomers born a lot earlier? The astronomers named the first five planets to be discovered; Venetia named the ninth. They chose the names of ancient gods: Mercury, Venus, Mars, Jupiter, and Saturn. so did she: Pluto. Some wanted to name this tiny, hard-to-spot planet after Percival Lowell, who died before he could prove its existence. But Venetia suggested Pluto, the god of the murky underworld who wore a helmet that made him invisible . . . and her name stuck!

Why don't planets bump into each other? ▼

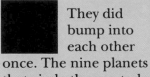 They did bump into each other once. The nine planets that circle the sun today are the ones that won the bumping contest.

When our solar system began forming 4.5 billion years ago, swarms of tiny planets, called planetesimals, orbited the sun. Some smashed into each other and be-

came space dust, others collected together to form larger planets. These planets then "absorbed" the planetesimals that ran into them, and grew bigger.

Finally, the nine biggest planets had swept clean pathways for themselves around the sun. And they're still following those bump-free orbits today.

Why is Venus hotter than Mercury when it's farther from the sun?

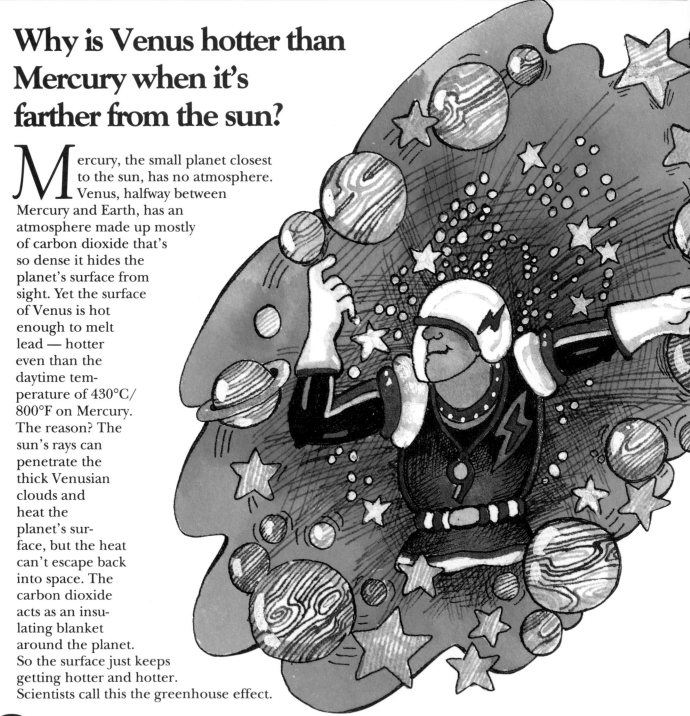

Mercury, the small planet closest to the sun, has no atmosphere. Venus, halfway between Mercury and Earth, has an atmosphere made up mostly of carbon dioxide that's so dense it hides the planet's surface from sight. Yet the surface of Venus is hot enough to melt lead — hotter even than the daytime temperature of 430°C/800°F on Mercury. The reason? The sun's rays can penetrate the thick Venusian clouds and heat the planet's surface, but the heat can't escape back into space. The carbon dioxide acts as an insulating blanket around the planet. So the surface just keeps getting hotter and hotter. Scientists call this the greenhouse effect.

Illustration © Danielle Jones 1989

Why does Saturn have rings?

Scientists believe that Saturn's rings have two causes. First, they think that two of Saturn's moons collided and broke up into pieces. Second, those pieces kept smashing into each other to produce smaller and smaller pieces. That process continued until finally what was left was trillions of pieces of material that now form the rings around Saturn. By the way, if you managed to get hold of one of those pieces and bring it home you'd discover it was made of . . . ice!

Do other planets have sunrises and sunsets?

Yes, but you could see them only on Mercury, Mars and Pluto because these planets aren't shrouded in dense, hazy atmospheres. The length of day differs on all these planets because they rotate at different speeds. Earth rotates once every 24 hours, so the sun sets at the equator 12 hours after it rises. Mercury rotates once every six months! Sunset happens three months after sunrise on this planet. That's a long, hot day — the sun looks three times larger than it does from Earth. A Martian day is almost the same length as ours, but the sun appears one-third smaller. On Pluto, which rotates once every six and a half days, the sun sets three days and four hours after it rises. But since the sun is so far away, it simply looks like a dazzling star in a permanently black sky. A day on Pluto is only as bright as dusk on Earth.

H--w many star are there in the Milky Way Galaxy? ▼

Our home galaxy, the Milky Way, is a city of stars – perhaps as many as 200 billion of them. The sun is merely one star among all those billions. The Milky Way is a spiral galaxy, shaped a bit like a Frisbee. Earth is inside the "Frisbee," about half-way between one edge and the middle. That's one reason why every star you can see from Earth belongs to our galaxy. How many can you see? If you're star-gazing in the city, you'll be lucky if you can see 200. Away from lights, however, you might see as many as 4,000.

Can you ever see rainbows at night?

Rainbows *do* happen at night, although they are usually much harder to see than those that color the daytime sky. Next time you see bright moonlight shining down upon falling water, look closely. You may be able to spot faint nighttime rainbows. Two huge African waterfalls are famous for their mysterious moonbows. Moonbows? They're like rainbows, only they're made from moonbeams, not sunbeams.

Why do stars twinkle?

It's because they're so far away. Our nearest star after the sun is so distant that its light reaches Earth as a tiny pinpoint. Any movement of air in our atmosphere causes this pinpoint of light to waver, or twinkle. You can use this fact to decide if you're watching a star or planet, because planets don't twinkle. The light from a planet reaches Earth as a much bigger bundle of light because it's close enough to be seen as a disc, not merely a pinpoint. The larger the bundle of light, therefore, that reaches Earth, the less it's affected by our turbulent atmosphere and the more constant it appears to us. Besides, "Twinkle, twinkle little planet" just doesn't sound right!

Is there such a thing as stardust?

Yes. When a star explodes, pieces of the star blast out into space. Some of this "stardust" is as small as earth dust; some of it is the size of boulders. The stardust floats around until it's sucked into another star or enough of it gathers together to form a new planet. Scientists believe that Earth might have been formed when flecks and chunks of stardust swirled together into a ball. If you'd like to see some stardust for yourself, look under your bed. Chances are there's some stardust in among the other bits of dust you'll find there, because Earth still picks up more than 1,000 tons of stardust a day as it travels through space.

Are there really only seven colors in a rainbow?

Everyone learns the rainbow's colors as ROYGBIV — red, orange, yellow, green, blue, indigo and violet, with red at the top and violet at the bottom.

But the colors don't come in seven clearly marked bands. Each color blends slowly into the next, creating a whole array of subtle colors. And there are at least two bands of color that your eyes can't see. Scientists with special cameras have discovered invisible infrared light above the red band and equally invisible ultraviolet light below the violet band. So ROYGBIV should really become IROYGBIVU!

Why aren't rainbows white like sunlight?

The fact that raindrops can bend light is crucial to the creation of a multi-colored rainbow. Why? Light is made up of many colors, and they all bend differently. Violet light bends more than green, which in turn bends more than red. So when these colors bounce back out of the raindrop, they're all heading in slightly different directions. These differences are small, but they're enough so that by the time the light reaches your eyes, the colors have spread out in the familiar rainbow pattern.

Why can't there be a pot of gold at the end of a rainbow?

Sorry, but it's impossible to find a pot of gold at the end of a rainbow. This isn't necessarily because there is no pot of gold. It has more to do with the elusive nature of rainbows. First of all, a rainbow is a reflection, not a solid object. And secondly, a rainbow is only part of a perfect circle, which of course, has no end. Ah well!

How is a rainbow made?

Rainbows are made out of sunlight and rain. The falling rain forms a sheet of billions of drops of water. Think of this sheet as being like a trick mirror in a midway funhouse — the one with curved glass. The mirror is curved so that the reflection is aimed at one place, which is why you don't see your reflection unless you stand in the right place.

Raindrops act like curved mirrors. Sunlight hits the raindrops, bounces once inside them and is reflected out. But it doesn't come out helter-skelter. It's concentrated at a particular angle, almost like a flashlight beam. When you look at the right place in the sky, you see each beam of light from all those raindrops coming together to make a rainbow.

WILD AND NOT-SO-WILD LIFE

Come on back down to Earth and ponder things closer to home — like pets, for example. Ever wonder why a cat sometimes purrs and acts mean at the same time? If it's happy, your cat makes purring sounds. It can purr when it's anxious, too. So, if your cat is nervous or frightened, it might purr and try to protect itself by lashing out with well-sharpened claws. At other times, your cat will purr because it enjoys playing a game with you. But if you touch its sensitive belly, your cat will grab you with its paws and teeth. It thinks it's only playing, but it can hurt you without meaning to.

Do cats make you sneeze? Some people are allergic to the small scales on cat (or dog or rabbit or horse) hair that's called dander. Dander sticks to carpets and furniture. That's why you might be sneezing even when a cat's nowhere to be seen. But it can work both ways. Did you know that a cat might be allergic to you — especially if you're wearing something like perfume or hair spray? Some of the ingredients in these things can cause allergies in cats. Like you, cats can be allergic to pollen, house dust, chicken, fish — and even dogs!

While we're on the topic of dogs, have you ever noticed how a dog will prick up its ears before you hear anything? Dog's ears are like wide, rotating satellite dishes. Dogs raise and swivel their ears to locate sounds too faint for humans to hear, like someone whistling around a corner and down the block. Dogs can also hear many sounds that are too high-pitched for us, such as a bat's squeak.

EEEP!

The mention of bats brings us to wilder life. You probably know that a bat is the only mammal that flies. As a mammal, a mother bat gives birth to a live baby. But did you ever wonder *how* she does it? Just before birth, the mother bat finds a comfortable nursery roost. Because she hangs upside-down, holding on to the roost with her feet, she has no "hands" to catch her baby as it comes out. Instead, she counts on a strong, flexible membrane attached to her tail, which acts as a safety net for the newborn baby bat.

Speaking of babies . . . ever wonder how a chick can breathe when it's inside an egg? An eggshell looks as though it's made of one solid piece of shell. But it's actually full of about 8,000 tiny holes. Each hole, called a pore, has a funnel shape that allows oxygen to enter the shell without the insides leaking out.

And what about underwater wonders — like the octopus? An octopus' body is not like yours. It's made up of a large bag that narrows into a small head. Although the bag looks like the octopus' head, the brain, the eyes and the mouth are all found at the bottom of the bag where the arms join. Inside the large bag, there's a smaller sac that contains the stomach, heart and other organs. In between the big bag and the smaller sac is a space that collects sea water through a tube called a siphon. When the octopus squeezes the bag, water squirts out through the siphon and sends the octopus off like a rocket. And if the octopus needs more than speed to escape an enemy, it squirts ink from a gland inside its body to create a smoke screen. That's quite a bag of tricks!

For many more surprising facts about the bodies and behaviors of wild animals, pets and plants, read on.

Why don't dogs' noses freeze outside in winter? ▶

The secret to a dog's frost-resistant nose lies beneath its skin: a network of tiny, hard-working blood vessels. More warm blood gets pumped here than anywhere else in the dog's body. So even though a dog's nose is wet, it never gets cold enough to freeze because of the non-stop warmth beneath its skin.

How do snakes move?

To move in a straight line, snakes use their belly scales, called "scutes," to grip the ground, a bit like treads on snow tires. Then, by shortening muscles attached to the scutes, they can pull themselves forward *inside* their skin. As soon as their belly scales release their grip, the skin moves forward too. This straight-line movement is called "creeping." Snakes can also move in S-bends, by twisting their backbones as they push off soil, sand or plant stems.

Why do mice have such long tails?

A mouse depends on that long, skinny tail. Mostly it's used for balance when the mouse is sitting up on its hind legs, jumping, or climbing a tree. Also, a mouse can hold itself steady by wrapping its tail around a twig or a blade of grass. On hot days, a mouse keeps its tail extended so that blood flowing near the skin can cool off. On cold days, a mouse wraps its tail around its body to help keep it warm . . . kind of like a mouse muffler!

Why does my goldfish hit the sides of its bowl?

Bump! Your goldfish can't easily distinguish between the glass and the water, so it has to use its sense of touch. Also, the edge of the bowl and the water may create an optical illusion that makes it difficult for your goldfish to tell the difference between the two. Dark paper taped to an outer wall may help your pet locate this side less painfully.

Why does my budgie fly into the wall when I let it out of the cage?

Your budgie doesn't have much room in a cage to master the difficult art of flying. It has to learn how to turn, bank, ride air currents and do many other things it can't practice in a small space. And since it's not used to wide open spaces it may have problems judging distance. But if you can let your budgie out of its cage more often, you'll quickly see it develop into a flying ace.

Why doesn't it hurt a kitten when its mother picks it up by the neck?

All cats have very sharp teeth, but the mother cat knows just how firmly she can pick up her kitten so that she won't bite into its skin. She also is careful to pick it up by the furry "handle" of loose skin around the kitten's neck. Because the kitten is so light, there's not much weight pulling down on this handle. Also, almost all cats instinctively stop moving when they're picked up by the loose skin around the neck.

Do pets watch TV?

It's unlikely your cat will become a rock video fan or your dog will turn into a soap opera addict, but animals do watch TV. Even though they see little or no color, cats and dogs are attracted to the movement they see on TV, probably because of their hunting instincts. Perhaps the action reminds them of small scurrying animals. But the main reason they watch TV is to keep you company. Most pets also like music and some even join in and "sing" along.

103

How do mice squeeze through such small holes?

A tiny house mouse has a sleek, small body, light, flexible bones and stretchy ligaments that let it scrunch, stretch and squeeze its body through holes smaller than a 25-cent piece!

Are mice always timid?

Most mice are quiet, gentle little creatures that prefer to avoid confrontations. But there are some mice that are so aggressive they might even scare off Mighty Mouse. They're known as grasshopper mice, and they live in the central and western regions of the U.S. They look like ordinary cute field mice, but they've earned the nickname of killer mice! These ferocious predators attack large insects, scorpions, even other mice — tearing them apart as they eat them. They even throw back their heads and pierce the air with their calls, just like wolves.

How can mice be so quiet?

Rubbery paws let the mouse pad silently around, its claws help it to grip surfaces, even very steep inclines, and its long, agile tail can be roped around a stem of grass or a wire to help the mouse keep its balance. And this can all be done with scarcely a rustle.

Why do mice have such big ears?

A mouse's large, round ears act like swiveling satellite dishes to help it pick up sounds from all directions. A mouse can hear many sounds we can't, especially high-frequency sounds. Excellent hearing helps the mouse avoid being snatched up by fast-flying birds. It's a good thing that mouse ears can hear so well because mouse eyes don't see very well.

Are mice really always busy?

Most mice scurry around day and night all year round, searching out food and exploring their territory, pausing only for naps. But dormice, which live in Europe and Asia, fatten up on food during the summer. When fall comes, they nestle into a safe hideout and hibernate until May.

How do mice see in the dark?

Mice are nearsighted, so they can distinguish something moving only if it's close by. In the dark, the mouse relies on its sensitive hearing and its sensitive whiskers. They let the mouse know how close it is to walls or other mice, or whether it will be able to squeeze through a small hole. Whiskers give the mouse a 3-D picture of the world in the dark.

How do dogs smell so well?

Animals depend on their sense of smell much more than you do, and their noses show it. For instance, in each nostril you have barely enough smell cells to cover a small stamp. But in a dog's nose the smelling area is more than five times that big and packed with 20 times as many smell cells. Bloodhounds have such a keen sense of smell they can follow a trail several hours old.

Why do horses have "scabs" on their legs?

Those scab-like patches high on the insides of horses' legs are known as "chestnuts," and they're what's left of thumbs horses once had. The first horse ancestor was the size of a dog and had four toes per foot. Gradually, three of these toes fused into a hoof, which meant the horse could run faster. Once it had hooves, its thumbs – the fourth toes – were useless and slowly vanished, leaving only the chestnuts. They're high on the legs because as horses evolved their foot bones grew longer. How much longer? Take a look at your hand. A horse's front hoof is the same as the tip of your middle finger, its ankle compares to the knuckle at the base of that finger and its knee is the same as your wrist.

What's the difference between hair and fur?

In a sense there's no difference. Fur is made of densely packed hair – so fur is hair . . . and so are whiskers and quills. Some animals have two types of fur. They have a thick coat of short, fine hairs that insulates the body and an overcoat of long guard hairs that sheds water.

What's the hairiest animal alive? The musk ox wins hooves down. Its 1 m/ 3 foot-long hair keeps it warm no matter how cold the weather gets.

Why don't dogs' nails grow?

You might think that your dog's nails never grow, but the fact is they do! And some dogs' nails grow so long that they have to be taken to the vet to have them clipped. But really all a dog needs to keep its nails trim is a sidewalk. Walking on cement is like walking on nature's nail file.

Why can't fish close their eyes?

Fish don't have eyelids like yours. Your eyelids protect only when you blink or close your eyes to keep them wet and to wipe away dirt and dust and so on. That kind of protection isn't enough for a fish. Just as you put on a mask when you want to swim around and look at things underwater, so fish eyes have a clear covering that gives them constant protection.

Fish don't need eyelids like yours for other reasons. Since fish live in water their eyes are always wet. Also, things move more slowly in water than in air, so fish can dodge most dirt. And even if something does enter their eyes, it's not going fast enough to do much damage. To protect their eyes when they're racing towards their prey, sharks roll them back into their head, make a blind charge and, at the last second, unroll their eyes to see what's for dinner.

Why do some animals' eyes shine at night?

Animals that prowl around for food during the night need all the help they can get to be able to see. That's why most nocturnal, or night-active, mammals — such as deer, hyenas, skunks, porcupines, cats and dogs — have a shiny layer on the back inner surface of their eyes. This surface helps to reflect light back so the animal can see better in the dark. It's not just mammals that have this feature. Some species of fish, such as the tarpin, and some night-hunting spiders in Australia and Central and South America do too.

What animal has the biggest eyes in the world?

All squid have big eyes. But the rarely seen giant squid has eyes the size of an extra-large pizza. If you had eyes like the giant squid's, your face would have to be larger than a big wading pool to contain them. Talk about 20/20 vision!

How do fish see underwater?

It depends on the fish. Some fish use sunlight to see. In clear ocean waters, light can filter down to 300 m/1,000 ft. That's as deep as a 10-story building is tall! Other fish don't rely on sight. Instead they sense their environment, using whiskers, electric fields, smell and vibration.

Why do roosters crow in the morning?

Long ago when chickens were wild, roosters crowed so loudly to attract a mate that they were in danger of being pounced on by a predator looking for a chicken dinner. To avoid being seen, they began to do most of their crowing when the light was dim – in the early morning and late afternoon. Today's equally loud-mouthed roosters still crow most at those two times. But early in the morning you notice them more because there's usually not a lot of other noises going on then to distract you.

Why do dogs circle around before they lie down?

Your dog circles around to prepare a safe and comfortable "nest" for itself to sleep in. Sound strange? It's an old habit, practiced by wild dogs who circled around to make sure no predators were lurking and to trample down the grass to make their nest more comfy. Dogs aren't the only animals that have this kind of "nesting behavior." For example, some people plump up their pillows before they crawl into bed. What special way do you have of making your "nest" cozy too?

Why are cats so difficult to teach?

Cats aren't stupid. It's just that they've never learned to take orders like dogs have. Your dog's wild relatives lived in packs that were run by a pack leader. Your dog thinks of you as his pack leader, and instinctively wants to obey and please you. But your cat's wild relatives lived on their own and didn't take orders from anyone. And neither does your tabby.

How do worms see underground?

Worms don't have eyes like we do, so they have to feel their way around. Fortunately they move so slowly that they don't hurt themselves if they bump into something. At the surface, worms use light-sensitive organs on their heads and tails to detect harsh, bright sunlight that might dry them out. When they sense bright lights, they retreat back underground to the safety of darkness.

Why do fish lay so many eggs?

Because most fish lay their eggs in the open and don't stay around to protect them, they produce thousands of eggs, gambling that at least a few will survive. On the other hand, some fish don't need to lay so many eggs because they put them in safe places. Sticklebacks, for instance, make "nests" for their eggs, while female sea horses deposit their eggs in a special brood pouch on the male sea horse's belly.

Do fish sing?

Fish don't actually open their mouths and belt out a tune, but that doesn't stop them from using "fish songs" to communicate with each other. It's true, however, that fish singers are rare: of the 20,000 species of fish only 150 or so species are known to produce high-frequency sounds that we might call "songs."

GOBY FISH

Why do fish sing?

Fish aren't exactly tuneful, so you might well ask why they bother singing at all. Fish are practical creatures, so they don't sing for pleasure (as far as we know). They sing to get a message across, just as birds do. One song might mean "This territory is taken, please move on," another might mean "Time to change direction," and yet another "Let's get out of here." If you're a minnow, a blenny or a goby fish, of course, your song might mean "I'd make the perfect mate for you."

SEAHORSE

Can you sing like a fish?

Do you grate your teeth? If so, you can already sing like some fish. And if you can also grate your bones together, you can sing a song with a clownfish or a seahorse, because that's how they do it. Others, such as parrotfish, croaking gourami, filefish and puffers grate all kinds of things — teeth, fins and spines among them.

Have you ever made drumming sounds by patting your chest? If so, you can make noises that sound a little bit like the ones triggerfish and several others can make. Each plays its swim bladder "drum" by vibrating muscles that surround it or are attached to it.

W e're not sure how you can ever manage to sing like a barracuda, or a school of herrings, sardines or anchovies. Their sudden movements — a change of direction or swimming speed — create noises that sound like a low roar or a wooden mallet striking a boat underwater.

BARRACUDA

Can you hear a fish sing?

Next time you're out in a boat under the light of a silvery moon, listen carefully. Some fish get together for a night-time sing-song. Marine catfish, for instance, tend to sing together each summer, especially around the time of the new moon. Their chorus, which sounds a bit like a coffee percolator at full boil, starts at 5:00 p.m. and ends at 11:00 p.m. No late show for these ones. Another group of watery wailers, called sea robins, chirp to each other. And if you ever find yourself standing on the shore of any of the Great Lakes, listen for the sounds of freshwater drum fish. What do they sound like? You guessed it . . . drums!

TRIGGERFISH

MARINE CATFISH

Who's the best singer of them all?

It's too bad that the male oyster toadfish can't stand up and take a bow, because he's the star of the fish-singing world, even though he doesn't sing all that often. Since he tends to sing most during the late spring, scientists think that his boat whistle may be a mating call, since he usually makes it at the nest when he's ready to spawn. Although it's the oyster toadfish's boat whistle call that enthralls people and prompts them to compare it to a bird song, that's not the only sound he makes. He's great at grunting too.

OYSTER TOADFISH

How tall is a baby giraffe?

A newborn giraffe makes quite an entrance. Since the mother giraffe gives birth standing up, her calf literally drops into the world, falling 2 m/6½ ft. But even though it's about the same height and weight as a tall man, the calf is hidden away for a month or more. It reaches its full height by the time it's four, and continues to put on weight for another three or four years. For as long as it's still growing, it's protected by adult giraffes.

What's the biggest fish in the world?

Would you believe that the biggest fish in the world is a shark that is harmless to humans? The whale shark may grow to be one and a half times the length of a bus, yet it eats only plankton and small fish. So even though its jaws hold up to 4,000 teeth, each tooth is so tiny the whale shark will never replace its great white cousin as a movie star!

What's the biggest bird that can fly?

The heaviest flying bird is the Kori bustard that soars through the skies of eastern and southern Africa. It weighs as much as an 11-kg/30-lb, three-year-old child.

How big is a giant panda?

A giant panda isn't really a giant. At birth it isn't much bigger than a mouse. And when it's full grown it weighs about as much as a big man and is only about 1 m/3 ft tall at the shoulder. But one thing about the panda is giant — its appetite for bamboo. It eats about 27 kg/60 lbs of it daily. No wonder the giant panda spends almost all of its waking hours eating.

What's the biggest bug?

First we should make something clear. A bug is a specific kind of insect that has a special front-wing structure and a beak-like tool that it uses for feeding. Other insects do not have these features. Some common bugs that you might have seen are bedbugs, stink bugs, water boatmen and water striders. (Ladybugs and mealybugs are *not* true bugs.)

The biggest bug is the giant water bug. Common in ponds across North America, this dark brown creature can grow to a length of just over 50 mm/2 in. The South American species is twice that length! The giant water bug gets that big by eating insects, snails, tadpoles and even small fish. It grabs them with its front legs, sticks in its beak and sucks out their juices.

When it's had enough of the water, the giant water bug spreads its wings and flies about. If you're lucky you might see one hovering around your porch light on a hot summer night.

By the way, the biggest flying *insect* is the Goliath beetle — it tips the scales at 100 g/3 ½ oz.

Bug-Eyed Quiz

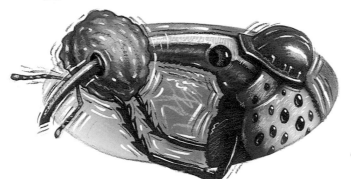

1. Some ants are gardeners. They cut leaves and take them to underground chambers, where they use them as mulch to grow fungus.

True ☐   **False** ☐

2. Monarch butterflies feed on poisonous milkweed plants, so birds leave them alone. Viceroy butterflies don't feed on poisonous plants, but birds leave them alone too because they look a lot like monarchs.

True ☐   **False** ☐

3. Insects were the very first creatures on Earth that learned how to fly.

True ☐   **False** ☐

4. A baby dragonfly has gills and can breathe under water.

True ☐   **False** ☐

6 Fireflies aren't really flies, they are beetles.

True ☐   **False** ☐

7 More than half of all living things on Earth are insects.

True ☐   **False** ☐

5. The Hercules beetle from South America is as big as a mouse.

True ☐   **False** ☐

8 Some dragonflies can eat their weight in food every half hour.

True ☐   **False** ☐

9 The South American grasshopper not only looks like a stick but it also sways as though caught in a breeze.

True ☐   **False** ☐

10 Monarch butterflies fly from Canada to Mexico to spend the winter.

True ☐   **False** ☐

11 Only female deerflies bite; males dine on flowers.

True ☐   **False** ☐

12 Houseflies walk all over your food so they can taste it — they've got tastebuds on their feet.

True ☐   **False** ☐

13 Some weevils can drill holes in nuts with their snouts.

True ☐   **False** ☐

14 A bug called the water boatman swims on its back using its paddle-like third pair of legs.

True ☐   **False** ☐

15 Some tropical termites build their mud homes 6 m/18 ft high. An equivalent man-made building would be 4 km/2.5 mi high.

True ☐   **False** ☐

16 The antennae of green male midges act like CB radios, picking up the frequency of buzzing females.

True ☐   **False** ☐

17 One kind of queen termite lives for 50 years and lays 30,000 eggs a day.

True ☐   **False** ☐

18 Some cicadas spend 17 years underground before becoming winged adults.

True ☐   **False** ☐

Answers: All of the statements are true.

117

Why do spiders spin webs?

Spiders spin webs to trap insects to eat. The webs are made of silk that the spider manufactures in special silk glands in its abdomen. The webs most often found in houses are cobwebs. But in gardens you're likely to see orb webs. They look like bicycle wheels with radiating spokes. Although spider webs are strong enough to catch insects, they do get damaged. To repair a damaged web, spiders eat up the wrecked bits and spin new silk to repair the holes. If the damage is really bad, they'll eat up all the remaining bits and spin an entirely new web. Not all spiders spin a traditional web to trap insects. These four spiders, for example, have developed other ingenious ways to catch their lunch.

◀ The ogre-faced spider hangs upside-down holding a bug-catching net between its front legs. When an insect passes by, the ogre stretches open its net and sweeps it down over its victim.

Hyptiotes spins its triangular web, then holds on to one corner thread. When an insect flies into the web, Hyptiotes lets its thread go slack so that the web collapses around the insect in a tangled mess. ▼

◀ The bola spider sits quietly waiting for a tasty insect to fly by. When a victim comes near, the bola throws a ball of glue attached to a silken line. If its aim is good, its dinner sticks to the glue ball, and all the bola has to do is reel in dinner.

● Moths escape from most webs by shedding their wing scales. To trap them, the ladder web spider builds a long, escape-proof web. When a moth flies into this "ladder," it flip-flops down to the bottom, losing all its scales. Then it's stuck for good. ▶

Who's the biggest glutton in the animal kingdom?

The African bullfrog, and most of its cousins, would take the gold medal in this category. It gorges on tasty insects until its stomach is full, its throat is full, even its mouth is full. Sometimes it crams itself so full that tiny twitching insect legs stick out of its mouth.

Who can last the longest without food?

On land, the winner is the North American grizzly bear. It can hibernate for up to seven months without a bite of food by using up stored body fat. But that's nothing compared with the African lungfish. It can live without food or water for more than a year.

Who's the messiest eater?

You wouldn't want to sit next to a starfish at dinner. It pushes its stomach completely out of its body to cover its food. The meal is eaten and digested before the stomach is pulled back in.

Who's the weirdest eater?

When food gets scarce, the ribbon worm eats itself. No, it doesn't take bites out of its own body. Instead it uses up its organs, much the same way as a bear uses up stored body fat.

When food becomes plentiful, the ribbon worm replaces the parts it "ate" and becomes large and healthy again.

Who's the most fearless eater?

This one's a tie. Which do you think should win? The Egyptian plover, which lives along the sandy river banks of Central and Northeastern Africa, nips into the open mouths of crocodiles to feed. Some scientists think it's picking food from the croc's teeth, others think it's gobbling up leeches stuck on the reptile's tongue. The plover is up against a 13 cm/5-inch-long bullfrog that ate a 20 cm/8-inch-long alligator.

Who has the world's biggest appetite for little things?

It's a good thing the blue whale doesn't have to carry home the groceries. This huge mammal stretches as long as three city buses parked end to end. But it feeds entirely on tiny shrimp-like creatures called krill. In the summer, the blue whale fills up on as many as 3.6 tonnes/4 tons of these tiny taste treats a day.

Why do apples turn brown after you cut into them? ▶

When you cut through the skin of an apple, you expose its white flesh to the air. When that happens, naturally occuring phenolic compounds in the apple oxidize – mix with oxygen in the air and cause the exposed flesh to turn brown. This browning is the apple's natural defense mechanism. It stops the oxidization from destroying the rest of the apple, at least for a while. You can slow down the browning by soaking the apple in lemon juice. That stops the air from getting at the apple.

Why do jumping beans jump?

Jumping beans jump because there's something alive inside. A jumping bean is actually the seed of a Mexican shrub. Inside the seed is the larva of a tiny moth. When the seeds are left in a warm place, the larva starts to move around. And that causes the jumping bean to tumble and jump.

What's the oldest vegetable on earth?

t's hard to pin down the oldest vegetable on earth, but we do know that by 6000 BC people in the Near East were eating lentils. Scientists also believe that, halfway around the world, beans, peas, gourds and water chestnuts were being cultivated in the Far East, and that people living in what is now Mexico were growing gourds, beans and pumpkins. So when you start carving out faces next Halloween just think, pumpkins are almost 8,000 years old!

What kind of shells do cashews come in?

Before we get into a cashew's shell we should first tell you that a cashew isn't really a nut . . .it's a seed that grows on a tropical evergreen tree in Central and South America. Cashews are quite extraordinary.

They grow out of the end of a pear-shaped fruit called the cashew apple which is about three times as large as a cashew and is used to make jam. The cashew doesn't have a hard, leathery, "nutty" shell. Instead it's protected by two layers of casing. Cashews are related to mangoes and poison ivy. Raw cashews are poisonous. But roasting destroys the poison.

Is a tomato a fruit or a vegetable?

A tomato is a fruit. And if you want to be specific you can rightfully call it a "berry." It grows on a plant that's part of the nightshade family, so its cousins are eggplants, potatoes and tobacco. When tomatoes were first introduced into Europe people wouldn't eat them, because they thought they were poisonous.

Why do apples crunch?

Apples – and, for that matter, lettuce, celery and carrots – crunch because they're composed of cells that are filled with water. When you chomp into an apple, these cells explode and tiny spurts of water burst out. Those little explosions make that satisfying CRUNCH. How loud the crunch is depends on how strong the cell walls are. If the walls are strong and can take a lot of pressure (like those of an apple), the crunch is good and loud. If they're weak (like those of an orange), there's no real crunch at all.

How much water is in a watermelon?

Watermelons are perfectly named. They're 93% water. In a really big 45 kg/100 lb watermelon, the amount of water inside could weigh more than you!

Are all frogs green?

No. It's true that most frogs do have green markings, which they rely on for camouflage. But one small group of frogs are blue, orange, pink, yellow, red or brown. Why are they so brightly colored? It's their way of warning potential predators, such as birds, not to eat them.

This poison dart frog, for example, is so poisonous it doesn't need to hide from predators. In fact, no other animal produces a poison so deadly. Indians of Central and South America, where this frog lives, poison the tips of their hunting darts with the deadly secretions from its skin. That's how the frog gets its name.

Where do frogs lay their eggs?

Most frogs lay their eggs in water. However, some lay them on the ground, others lay them on leaves, and still others lay them underground. When it's time to lay their eggs, female African tree frogs select a branch over a pond or a swamp. Then they secrete a fluid, which the males help whip into a foam with their hind legs. After the females lay their eggs in this frothy nest, it forms a hard crust. A few weeks later the tadpoles break through the crust and drop to the water below.

Why do frogs croak?

Frogs croak to communicate . . . but not all frogs communicate by croaking. Some cluck, some bleat, some whistle, some scream. And the mating call of the male barking tree frog sounds more like a dog's bark than a croak. People claim that you can hear it 1.6 km/1 mile away! P.S. If you live or have traveled in the southern United States, you may have heard a barking tree frog. But unless you actually saw one, how would you know? Woof, woof.

Do all frogs live in ponds?

No. A few frogs live on the rain forest floor, others in sand dunes. The tree frog, however, leaves the pond it swam in as a tadpole and lives almost exclusively in . . . you guessed it, trees. The broad pads on its fingertips enable the frog to hold on tight so it can walk up tree trunks or hang from branches.

Are there any underwater forests?

If you could take a stroll through this underwater "forest" off the Pacific coast, you'd meet up with many small fish, birds and even sea otters. Why? This dense forest is made up of giant kelp plants. The plants are anchored to the sea floor and their leafy tops float at the surface. Many fish hide from predators in this forest. Harlequin ducks roost on it, and great blue herons use it as a fishing platform. Within the calm inshore water that is protected by the forest, gulls, loons, murres and other sea-birds can feed in safety. Even sea otters benefit. They wrap themselves in kelp as a safe anchor while they snooze. And not only does this forest protect all these animals, it also helps calm the seas and protect the shore from surging waves and pounding surf.

How long can a tree live?

A long, long time! Sitka spruce trees can live to be 700 years old. And England is home to 2 000-year-old yew trees. But they're just young things compared with bristlecone pines that grow in California. The oldest bristlecone on Earth is about 5 200 years old. That means it was already alive when the Egyptians built pyramids. What's the bristlecone's secret? Like other long-living trees, bristlecones are made to stand up against tough conditions — poor soil, little water, and constant winds. Their low height, five to 12 m (16 to 39 ft), helps protect them from high winds. Lots of resin, a sticky substance, keeps the bristlecones' wood from rotting. With these defences, they can't be beat. In fact, scientists think that the oldest bristlecone could live for another 1 000 years!

How high can sap be lifted up?

The force that raises sap up a tree is strong enough to lift it as high as 110 m/300 ft or more. That's taller than the Statue of Liberty!

How does a cactus get enough water in the desert?

The mighty saguaro cactus is built to beat the desert heat. Old saguaros can stand as tall as a three-story building. But unlike many trees whose roots would be as deep as the tree is tall, saguaros have a shallow root system. A three-story-tall cactus has roots covering an area of 30 m/ 100 ft in diameter and close to the surface so it can absorb rain as fast as it falls. Also, the waxy covering on the saguaro's skin reduces moisture loss by evaporation. Its pleats can expand like bellows as the spongy interior of the plant soaks up water. The moisture from one large rain-soaked saguaro could fill 100 bathtubs.

The saguaro's spines not only ward off would-be nibblers, they also help to break up the winds that rob the plant of moisture. And if a woodpecker drills a nest hole in a saguaro, the cactus seals off the wound with a "scab" to protect itself from water loss.

How do you eat a cactus?

C-a-r-e-f-u-l-l-y. Sometimes a land iguana from the Galapagos Islands follows this rule. It carefully scratches off the cactus's spikes so that it can munch on the soft parts. But other times it eats the cactus whole — spikes and all. The iguana must have cast-iron insides because the spikes pass right through and are excreted as waste.

Does the vampire bat suck blood?

Forget everything you've heard about Central and South American vampire bats sucking blood from cattle and horses. They don't. They lick up the blood from open wounds. Why doesn't the bat get caught by its prey? First of all, since its feet are padded and it only weighs about 40 g/ 1½ oz, the victim rarely feels the bat land. Also, the bat has razor-sharp teeth to make bites quick and painless. And it only takes about a large spoonful of blood at a time. Being a skilled blood burglar means the bat can come back to the same animal another day.

How many termites does it take to fill up an Australian numbat?

About 20,000 . . . it's no wonder the numbat spends most of its day searching for food. With its strong foreclaws and long tube-shaped tongue, getting termites is a breeze for the nimble numbat. While it gulps small termites and chews on larger ones, the numbat won't pass up a tasty meal of ants. A numbat, by the way, is the only Australian marsupial you'll see sniffing around for food during the day. The others prefer to dine at night.

Do any animals eat porcupines?

In North America, fishers are probably the only animals that make a meal of a porcupine. How do they avoid the quills? They flip the porcupine over so that its soft belly is exposed and it can't fight back. Then they tuck right in.

Sea urchins are a bit like porcupines of the sea. Not many animals will risk eating them for fear of getting a mouthful of spines. That's no problem, however, for the sea otters that live off the coast of British Columbia. These nimble-fingered animals pluck off the spines as you might pluck leaves off an artichoke to get at the good stuff inside.

■ How do bats fly?

It takes you approximately a second to say the word "bat." In this short time, a bat can flap its wings 10 times. No wonder you can't see it clearly.

Scott Altenbach's extraordinary stop-motion photographs reveal how the world's only flying mammal stays aloft and exactly how it flaps its wings to fly. These photographs of the fringe-lipped bat stop motion at one ten-thousandth of a second.

1 The start of a downstroke. This begins the movement of air that lifts the bat's body upwards.

2 The wings, continuing downwards, start to swivel forward.

3 Just before the downstroke is completed, the bat's body gets the maximum amount of lift to send it through the air.

4 Now the wings are about to begin an upstroke.

5 When the wings are folded in, there is little drag through the air.

6 Next is the start of an upward flick, which gives the bat's body even more lift.

7 When the flick is finished, the bat is ready to begin another downstroke.

8 The wing beat starts again.

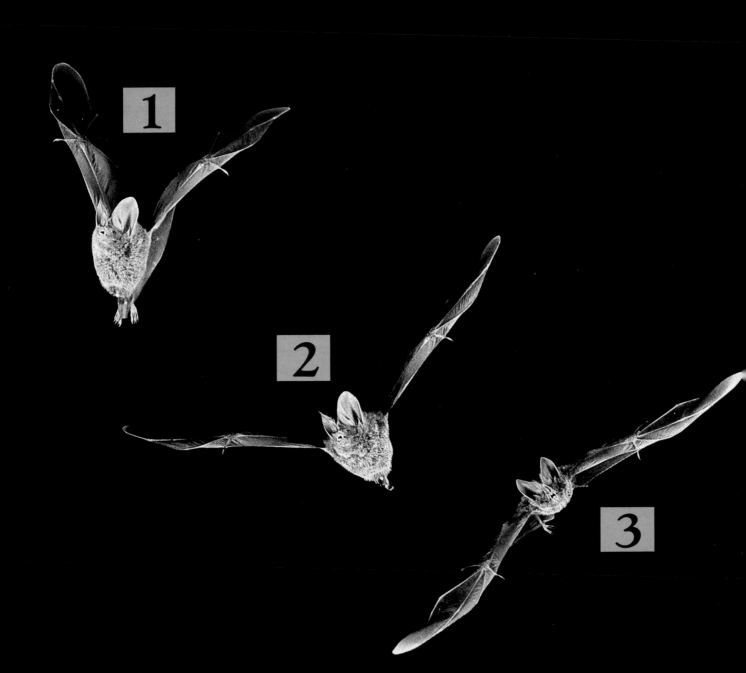

5

6

4

7

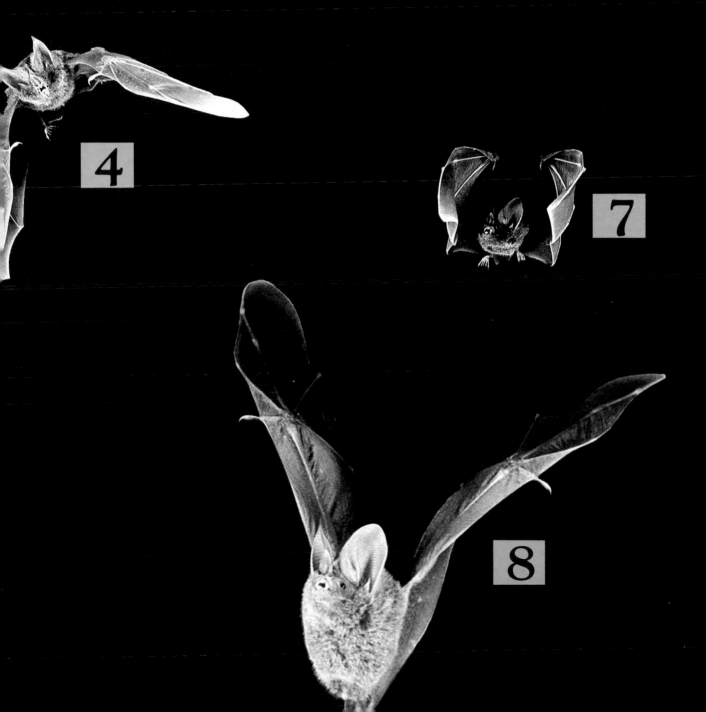

8

Why are ants so strong?

Why can an ant lift 50 times its weight while a human weight lifter can't manage 18 times his weight? It's because an ant's body is inside out compared to yours. Your muscles are attached around your bones, but an insect has an outer skeleton with its muscles inside. Its body is made up of hard tubes, and tubes are very strong structures. Unlike many insects, an ant can move its legs to be able to lift things.

Why don't electric eels get electrocuted?

For the same reason you don't when you move an arm. The electric eel has a set of protective coverings around its nerves that generate the same kind of electricity that you do every time you move a muscle. And just as you are grounded against the electricity you produce, so an electric eel is grounded against its own electricity . . . even though it lives in water.

The eel's electric organ runs down the eel's sides. The organ is made up of specialized muscles that can't contract like your muscles. What they can do, however, is work together to discharge electricity.

Normally the eel just puts out a little bit of electricity, which it uses to help it maneuver around and find food. The electric eel can increase its output for defense. The eel can emit an electric current of 650 volts, enough to stun even a horse.

The electric eel lives in the Amazon basin and is the most dangerous of all electric fish because it can repeat its stunning discharges several times an hour.

Why don't beavers get splinters in their mouths from chewing wood?

Beavers avoid the problem of splinters by never chewing dry wood. They chew down live trees, which are too full of sap to splinter. And in winter they store branches underwater, so these never have a chance of drying out either. Even if beavers did chew on dry wood, they'd still probably never get splinters in their mouths. Their big, furry lips close behind their huge orange front teeth so any splinters would be stopped right there. Beavers can also work very comfortably underwater without getting a single drop of water inside their mouths.

Can you charm a snake?

No, not really — you're just seeing a snake being a snake. When a snake charmer starts to play his flute, the snake, usually a cobra, rises out of its basket to check out the intruder in its territory. When the snake sees the flute player rocking back and forth in time to the music, it does the same. That's because male cobras rise up and follow each other's movements in a "challenge dance" when they meet. The cobra reacts to the snake charmer as if he's a snake. So the flute music isn't important, just the snake charmer's movements.

How do chameleons catch insects?

Unlike other lizards that usually chase after their prey, the chameleon slowly stalks the insects it eats for dinner. By creeping very slowly and changing its color to match the surrounding leaves, the chameleon avoids being spotted. When it gets about a body's length away from its meal, the chameleon suddenly flings out its long, slime-tipped tongue. The meal sticks to the tongue's tip and is then reeled in.

Why do slugs leave a trail of slime?

When a slug goes searching for juicy plants to eat, it glides on a trail of its own slime. How? The slug's long foot moves like a wave. When the slug puts down its "heel," the slime is sticky and glues the foot for take off. Then, as the foot ripples forward, the pressure causes the mucus-like slime to become more liquid and slippery so that the foot can slide along. Scientists are still baffled by how the slime changes back and forth from a solid to a liquid.

Why are fish slimy?

Without slime, fish would have a tough life. The water they swim in is full of parasites trying to latch on to any fish skin they can find. Slime to the rescue! It provides a shield that bacteria, fungi and algae can't penetrate. Fish continually secrete and shed slime to get rid of these parasites. It's like having disposable skin.

Why are frogs slimy?

Next time you struggle to catch your breath after a hard run, imagine how much easier it would be if you were a frog and could breathe through both your lungs and your skin. However, a frog's skin can only absorb oxygen that's dissolved in water. So frogs secrete mucus from glands just below their skin, and the slippery coating keeps water on the skin from drying up. A slimy frog is a healthy frog.

Are there any slimy mammals?

Since hippos live in the tropics they don't need fur, but they do need protection from the water they live in and from the hot sun. To get that protection, they ooze a red, oily, slimy substance from their skin. This helps to prevent the hippo's skin from wrinkling up like a prune when it stays in water for long stretches and from drying out on land.

Do animals have to take baths?

If you think this rhinoceros will need a bath after it's finished playing in the mud, think again. Why? It's actually wallowing in the bath this very moment. This might not look like a good way of getting clean to you, but mud wallowing gets rid of ticks and flies and cools the animal off. As a bonus, the mud coating protects the rhino's skin from the sun's harmful rays.

A giraffe has other ways of keeping clean. Since it isn't very easy for a giraffe to lie down to bathe, it relies on the rain to wash the dust of the African savannah out of its coat. And it depends on a little bird to pick out the ticks that get embedded in its hide. It's not unusual to see several tick birds, or oxpeckers, hard at work searching for insects on a giraffe's neck.

How does a snake stay clean?

The rat snake doesn't have to worry about staying clean. Although it spends all its time crawling around on the dirty ground, grime doesn't cling to its smooth skin. Even if it did, it wouldn't matter. In order to grow, snakes must shed their skin. So, about once a month, the snake sheds its old, dusty skin, emerging with a gleaming clean one. It even sheds its eye-coverings! As it sheds, the discarded skin is turned inside out. Lizards and other reptiles also keep clean by shedding their skin. It's a bit like throwing away all your clothes when they get dirty.

Do fish ever get dirty?

Even though fish swim around in water, they need an occasional clean-up too. In warm tropical seas, cleaner shrimp keep other fish clean by deftly nibbling off parasites. They also clean wounds. Even when the cleaner has to dig out parasites from below the skin, its fishy clients remain motionless. They even allow the shrimp into their gill covers and mouths. Talk about getting into your work!

Why do ▶ monkeys groom each other?

When someone shakes your hand, hugs you or even pats you on the back, they're trying to tell you something – that you're part of a group. Touching acts as "social glue" and helps keep groups together. Monkeys don't shake hands, but they do spend several hours a day grooming each other. This not only keeps them clean; it also helps to keep them together as a group, just as physical contact does among people.

Why does a rabbit wiggle its nose?

By wiggling its nose a rabbit can test air from many directions at once. This gives the rabbit a better chance of sniffing out any hidden enemies. But nose wiggling's not as easy as it looks. In fact, a rabbit is one of the few animals that has enough control over the nerves and muscles in its nose to be able to twitch the tip of it. Even though pet rabbits don't have to worry about enemies nearly as much as wild rabbits do, they still wiggle their noses; perhaps it lets them know when their owner is bringing them a treat.

Why do flies walk all over your food?

Flies don't walk all over your food just for the exercise. They do it so they can taste what they're about to eat. How? The tiny hairs on their feet act like the tastebuds on your tongue.

Why does my dog bark when I play the clarinet?

No offense meant, but your clarinet might sound like a howling dog. If so, your dog will instinctively bark and howl back. It's just good dog manners to do that.

Or perhaps you have trained your dog to bark without meaning to. For instance, if he starts to bark just as you begin to play the clarinet or when you hit a wrong note, you probably pay attention to him by laughing or patting him. By doing this, you reward him for barking. If the same thing happens again, your dog will quickly learn to howl when you play the clarinet. He figures he'll get lots of attention if he does!

How can cats lick dirt off their fur without gagging?

Although you'd probably gag at the thought of licking yourself clean every night, it doesn't bother a cat at all. Perhaps it has to do with the fact that cats have different taste buds than you do. You probably don't lick your lips when you see a dish of raw liver, but your cat will wolf it down and look for more. And a cat will likely turn up its nose at things that you consider treats — like cookies and cakes. If your cat licks you, she might like the salt on your skin.

Does my goldfish drink water?

Your goldfish drinks water, but not through its mouth. Instead, it absorbs water through its gills and skin. Watch a goldfish when it's feeding and you'll see that it tries to take in as little water as possible through its mouth. This is to prevent its blood — which has more salt in it than the surrounding water — from becoming diluted with fresh water. The fish absorbs the salt from the water as the water passes across its gills during breathing. Then it pumps out the excess water it doesn't need.

Saltwater fish, of course, have the opposite problem. Because there's so much salt in the water around them, they gulp down all the water they need through their mouths. Then they get rid of the salt through their gills or with their body wastes.

Why does my budgie mumble to itself?

Put several budgies together and they'll mutter, chirp and mumble all day long. They're no doubt communicating with each other, although it's difficult to tell what they're saying when they mutter. Chances are your budgie is a sociable little bird who's mumbling to you as if you were another budgie. If you've got a lone budgie for a pet, perhaps you should consider getting it a companion. Or perhaps you could just mumble back!

Why does a wood-pecker hammer on trees? Does it hurt? ▶

A woodpecker hammers on trees to get at its lunch. How does it know where to drill? It listens. Clinging to the bark, the woodpecker listens for bark beetles or larvae boring holes in the tree. When it hears them, the woodpecker starts drilling. Once it gets close to its dinner the woodpecker extends its long tongue into the hole and pulls out the food.

All that hammering doesn't hurt the woodpecker, because it's well built to withstand such action. It has a very thick skull, extra-large muscles in its neck and around its skull, and a very stiff tail, all of which help to absorb and cushion the blows.

Why does my dog stretch whenever I come in?

When your dog meets you at the door in this posture, it's not stretching, it's saying, "Hello, glad to see you." At any other time this posture means "Please play with me." If you want to play, get down on your knees, stretch out your arms and let your dog know.

Why does my cat yawn all the time?

If your cat yawns around you, don't be insulted. All it's saying is, "I'm relaxed around you." Yawn back or blink slowly and you'll give your cat the same message.

Why do chickens peck each other?

How is a group of chickens like a large corporation? They both have "pecking orders" that keep the group organized and running smoothly. In a big corporation, there's usually a boss, a second in command and so on down the line. Chickens use the same system, but in their case there's a lot of real pecking involved. Here's how it works. The "boss" chicken can peck all the birds below it. Bird number 2 can peck all but the boss. Bird number 3 can peck all but the boss and number 2, and so on down the line. All that pecking keeps even the most rebellious chicken in line.

Why do elephants ▼ trumpet?

Elephants trumpet for the same reasons that you yell. They do it when they're excited, surprised or want to warn another elephant of danger. They also trumpet when they're lost or about to attack. Elephants communicate in other ways too. They let members of their herd know that they are near and everything is safe by producing low rumbles in their bellies. A female elephant may call her young to her by noisily slapping her ears against her head. And some scientists think that elephants can communicate with such low sounds that humans feel them rather than hear them. Next time you're at a zoo, try to listen in on an ultra-low elephant conversation.

Do prairie dogs really bark?

Yes. In fact, prairie dogs are one of the animal world's most precise communicators. If an eagle swoops overhead, for example, they use their bark to alert the rest of the town that danger is nearby. All the prairie dogs that hear the warning signal immediately dive underground. It's thought that prairie dogs give a different call for as many as nine different enemies. And barks aren't the only sound prairie dogs make. They chitter when they're frustrated or mad, they chuckle when they're happy, they scream in pain or fear and they snarl when they're fighting.

How do dolphins whistle?

Imagine talking through your nose! That's what the dolphin does. It breathes in air through its blowhole when it's at the surface. Then, when it wants to talk to other dolphins, it moves "lips" inside the blowhole and makes squeals, whistles and clicks.

Why do rabbits thump?

Did you ever wonder why Bambi's friend Thumper thumped? When rabbits, and for that matter some hares, sense danger, they thump with their king-sized feet probably to warn others.

Why are flowers different colors?

Today we breed flowers in a whole rainbow of colors. But in the wild, flowers grow in different colors to attract certain birds and insects to help pollinate them. If a flower wants a bee pollinator, for instance, it will have better luck if it is yellow or blue. Those are the colors bees prefer. Moths like pale-colored flowers, while birds and butterflies are attracted to bright colors. Why are there so few green flowers in the wild? It seems that not many birds or insects like the color green.

How does a sprouting seed know which way is up?

Seeds respond to gravity just like you do. How? Little granules in the growing tips react to gravity and help orient the seedlings' growth. That's why no matter which way a seed is planted, it always manages to snake its root and shoot around so that the root grows down and the shoot grows up. Plants depend on gravity for their directions so much that when they're put into zero-gravity tanks, they get confused and grow any which way. This means that space gardeners will have to grow their plants in artificial gravity or be prepared to teach them which way is up.

How much paper does one tree make?

You could make a stack of newspapers about 1.3 m/4 feet tall from one average-sized tree. Does that seem like a lot of news to you? Well, here's some more news: the most massive living thing in the world is still alive and well in California . . .and it's a giant sequoia tree. More than 20 children holding hands could barely manage to circle it. And not only that, but there's enough wood in one giant sequoia to make 50 average-sized houses.

Which tree has the longest roots?

It depends on the kind of roots. Some trees have a long, tapered "tap" root that looks like an underground trunk. The longest tap root ever found belonged to an enormous fig tree in South Africa and went straight down 133 m/400 feet. Other trees, such as the oak, have surface roots that fan out underground in the same shape as the branches you see above ground. So the next time you're lying under a tree, looking up at the sky, just imagine how many roots you're lying on.

Do plants react when you talk to them?

Yes, but not because they find what you say particularly interesting. Plants have no sound receptors or nervous systems, so they can't hear you or detect the vibrations your voice makes. But when you talk you produce two things that plants really do react to. You breathe out carbon dioxide and water – two of the major necessities of life for all plants. So to keep your plant healthy, give it light, water and TLC (that's tender, loving chat).

Do all flowers open in the morning?

For most living things, light is like an alarm clock. It tells us when to wake up and when to go to bed. Like people, most flowers "awaken" and open their petals during the daylight. That way bees and other daytime creatures can help spread their pollen. But some flowers, such as the evening primrose, are night owls. They stay closed all day and only "wake up" at night.

How much water does a tree raise from its roots to its leaves in a day?

The giant oak can raise seven bathtubs full of water per day!

Do animals get tanned? ▲

When they wake up on a bright sunny morning, most animals don't get out the beach towels and suntan lotion, because they are so furry they couldn't get a tan even if they wanted to. But some animals do lie around in the sun for other reasons.

Ring-tailed lemurs sunbathe in groups, before breakfast, standing up with their arms outstretched. They do it because they have poor blood circulation. If they didn't soak up the sun's warmth every morning, they would end up with a bad case of cold hands and feet.

To survive in the scorching desert heat, camels face into the sun whenever possible. That way the least possible amount of their body surface is exposed to the sun's burning rays.

Do animals get sunstroke?

Hot cows get cranky and can easily become sick. But finding shade on the prairies, where trees are scarce, can be a problem. To keep their cows cool, some prairie farmers wheel enormous slatted sunshades out into the fields. Although the slats let some sun through, they also allow the air to keep moving, which keeps the cows cool.

Can animals get sunburned?

Animals that don't have fur often need protection from the sun. Elephants, for example, go through a two-step process to prevent getting sunburned. After rolling in the mud they spray themselves with trunkfuls of dust. The dust sticks to the mud and protects the elephants' skin from the sun's harmful rays. It also makes a sandpaper coating that squishes unwanted bugs when the elephant rubs against a tree.

How did sheep survive the heat before people sheared them?

Very well, thanks to their thick, fleecy wool that keeps out not only the cold but the heat too! Even on the hottest day, the wool close to a sheep's skin can be more than 11°C/20°F cooler than its outer wool. Why else do sheep need fleece? It's loaded with oily lanolin, so rain runs off the top layer the way water runs off a duck's feathers.

Why don't mountain sheep slip?

Leaping from boulder to boulder on steep mountain slopes isn't at all scary for mountain sheep. Their hooves are split into two toes that can spread apart and grip uneven surfaces. On the bottom of each hoof is a soft pad that helps absorb the impact of hard landings and gives the sheep a non-slip contact with the ground. Although most domestic sheep no longer leap around mountain slopes, they still have the same split hoof as their wild relatives.

Why do sheep follow the leader?

You may think sheep are stupid because they are always ready to follow the leader. Yet following a leader makes sense if you're a sheep. In the wild, there's safety in numbers, and older sheep can also show young ones where to find the best food.

Why do some sheep's horns curl?

A sheep's horns curl because of the way they grow. Usually the outside surface of the horn grows more quickly than the inside, so the horns curl under. How fast the horns grow depends on the sheep's diet. If there's lots of food to munch on, the horns grow more than in a lean year when there's not much food. By the way, to tell the age of a sheep you count the number of rings on its horns. Telling its age is not what a sheep uses its horns for, though. Males use them to determine who's the leader and to attract a mate. Females use them for defense.

Does a baby hedgehog have spines?

Sometime from May to September, in Europe, Asia and Africa, baby hedgehogs are born in a safe, soft, warm, well-lined nest. At birth their eyes and ears are closed and they have no fur . . . they don't even have spines. Their spines are hidden just beneath the skin, which is swollen with fluid. This swelling prevents the spines from piercing the skin and hurting the mother during birth. Soon after birth, the fluid is absorbed by the baby's body and the 150 or so white spines poke through.

What animal has the most babies?

The house mouse takes the medal for the number of mammal babies: up to 32 in some litters. But that's nothing compared to the ocean sunfish, which lays up to 30 million eggs. Since the female just lays her eggs as she swims along and doesn't protect them, many of the eggs are eaten up by other fish. It's a good thing only a few ocean sunfish make it to adulthood. Why? Ocean sunfish are enormous, weighing up to 1,000 kg/2,200 lbs.

Why doesn't a baby kangaroo fall out of its mother's pouch?

A kangaroo's deep, upward-opening pouch is ideal for a hopping, grass-eating animal. The joey can't fall out no matter how fast its mother travels. And when the mother leans forward to graze, her baby can nibble on grass too, without even leaving the safety of her pouch! When the joey is about eight months old, its mother encourages it to get out and explore. She relaxes her pouch and out tumbles her baby. When the joey has had enough of the outside world, its mother spreads her legs, lowers her pouch, and her baby somersaults in headfirst.

How big is a baby elephant?

When it is born, a healthy male Sri Lankan elephant can weigh as much as 138 kg/304 lbs — that's heavier than the combined weight of more than 40 human babies. And that enormous size is matched by an unbelievable appetite. Baby elephants drink the equivalent of 15 large cartons of milk a day! With an appetite like that, it's no wonder the baby gains more than a kilo/2 ⅕ lbs every single day for the first little while. By the time it is one year old, it is four times heavier than it was at birth.

Do any animals give birth to identical twins?

Imagine the confusion that must face the nine-banded armadillo mother. Every spring, when she gives birth, she always has four identical babies that are all the same sex. At birth their skin is soft and leathery, but in a few weeks it hardens into bony body armor.

Are March hares really mad?

The March hare in *Alice in Wonderland* might have been mad during the month of March, but most hares act crazy from March right through till May. That's the mating season. During that time the hares might fight. And that's not all. Their hopping, running and chasing antics are enough to make the March hare look sane!

What's the difference between hares and rabbits?

If you can't tell the difference between hares and rabbits, you're not alone. Here's how the experts know who's who. Hares tend to be bigger than rabbits and have longer ears and legs. Also, hares molt twice a year and change color, while rabbits never change color. Finally, at birth hare babies are covered with hair and can see. Rabbit babies, however, are born hairless and can't see at all. Got it now? Okay — who's in the picture at the right, a rabbit or a hare?

How fast can a rabbit run?

Hares are some of the speediest animals around. The white-tailed jackrabbit, which is actually a hare, can hit speeds of up to 72 km/h/45 mph for short periods. It can leap 6 m/20 ft straight up into the air to keep an eye on pursuing predators.

Why do rabbit tracks look as if they're going backwards?

Next time you see a rabbit running quickly, watch it carefully. First it puts its small front feet down, usually one in front of the other or sometimes side by side. Rabbits' front legs are great for helping it to keep balanced or change direction. But they're too short to keep up with its long back legs. So when a rabbit runs fast, its back legs overtake its front ones and its big hind paws thump the ground in front of them.

What's the bump on a king vulture's beak for?

The nose ornament on the adult male King Vulture has nothing to do with smell and lots to do with looking good. It's what makes him look attractive to female vultures. Both the *caruncle*, the fleshy part on the bill near the nostrils, and the *wattle*, found near the eyes, become brighter in color during breeding season to show he's ready to mate. According to the legends of Mexico and South America, where this bird is found, its golden bump looked like a crown — and that's why it's known as the king of vultures.

INDEX

CONSULTANTS

For their expert advice, we would like to thank the following: Dr. J. F. Alex, Department of Environmental Biology, University of Guelph; Dr. R. Anderson; Dr. D. B. Bonder, Humber Equine Clinic; Dr. Dale Calder, Department of Invertebrate Zoology, Royal Ontario Museum; Dr. David Carr, McMaster University Medical Centre; Dr. D. Chute, Department of Life Sciences, University of Toronto; Dr. B. Colman, Department of Biology, York University; D.H. Cormack, Department of Anatomy, University of Toronto; Dr. I. G. Currie, Department of Mechanical Engineering, University of Toronto; Jim Dick, Department of Ornithology, Royal Ontario Museum; Terry Dickinson , Astronomy Specialist; Dr. G. Drake; Dr. James Eckenwalder, Department of Botany, University of Toronto; Dr. D. Ellis, Department of Otolaryngology, University of Toronto; Dr. J. Grayson, Department of Physiology, Faculty of Medicine, University of Toronto; Arthur Grosser; Elizabeth Gullett, University of Guelph; Ross James, Department of Ornithology, Royal Ontario Museum; Dr. B. R. Krafchik, Associate Professor, Faculty of Medicine, University of Toronto; Dr. Gary Landsberg, Thornhill, Ontario; Dr. P. J. Lea, Department of Anatomy, University of Toronto; Professor George Lewis, McMaster University Medical Centre; Jim Lovisek, Toronto Nature Centre; Ross MacCulloch, Department of Ichthyology and Herpetology, Royal Ontario Museum; Elizabeth MacLeod; Bob McDonald, science writer and broadcaster; Dr. Hooley McLaughlin, Ontario Science Centre; Paul McManus; Dr. K. G. McNeill, Department of Physics, University of Toronto; David Philipps, Environment Canada; Dr. Betty Roots, Chairman, Department of Zoology, University of Toronto; Dr. R. Schemenauer, Environment Canada; Dr. Paul Siswerda, New York Aquarium Animal Department; Dr. M. Schlesinger; Dr. Thomas Swatland, Department of Animal and Poultry Science, University of Guelph; Dr. Carol Swallow, Department of Surgery, Toronto General Hospital; Dr. M. Taylor, D.V.M., Martin Veterinary Hospital; Dr. J. M. Toguri, Department of Metallurgy and Materials Science, University of Toronto; Dr. Stephen Wallace, Department of Chemistry, University of Toronto; Susan Woodward, Department of Mammalogy, Royal Ontario Museum.

Special thanks to Nyla Ahmad, editor-in-chief of OWL and *Chickadee* Magazines, Sylvia Funston, former editor-in-chief of OWL and *Chickadee* Magazines, Debora Pearson, former editor of OWL Magazine, and Tim Davin, OWL's art director, as well as to those contributing writers who worked with them in answering the questions: Sheila Fairley, Katherine Farris, Linda Granfield, Susan Hughes, Jay Ingram, Elin Kelsey, Paula Kent Kuchmey, Bob Loeffelbein, Elizabeth MacLeod, Cynthia Pratt Nicolson, Sharon Siamon, Deena Waisberg and Lauren Wolk.

PHOTO AND ILLUSTRATION CREDITS

Pp. 2–3, 28–29, 102–103, 108–109, Nigel Dickson; 6–7, 52–53, 82–83, 100–101, Dave Whamond; 8–9 Terry Shoffner; 10–11, 19, 30–31, 36–37, 38–39, 59, 64–65, 74–75, 78–79, 140, Ray Boudreau; 11, Martine Bourbault; 12–13, 14–15, 16–17, 20–21, 24, 32–33, 34–35, 44–45, 48, 54–55, 60, 66–67, 68, 70–71, 72, 76–77, 80–81, 96–97, 106–107,122–123, Tony Thomas; 18–19 Hugh MacMillan Medical Centre; 21, 25, 26, 29, 33, 34, 37, 49, 61, 81, 85, 94–95, 107, 143, 148–149, Tina Holdcroft; 22–23, 42–43, Nicholas Leibrecht; 26–27, Shun Sasabuchi; 38, 39 (spots), Dan Hobbs; 40, Ken Sherman/Bruce Coleman Inc.; 41, Vesna Krstanovich; 47, 74, 95, 144, Danielle Jones; 50–51, Maryann Kovalski; 56–57, Robert Isear/Science Source; 58–59, Linda Sanborn; 58, Helen D'Souza; 62–63, 132–133, Laurie Lafrance; 66, Val Fraser; 78–79 (cartoon), Ross MacDonald; 84–85, David Edmonds; 86, 88–89, 92–93, NASA; 90, Terence Dickinson; 93 (spot), Gary Clement; 98–99, Ron Berg; 104, Tony Stone Worldwide/Masterfile; 105, Steve Attoe; 110–111, Greg McEvoy (Tyler*Clark); 112–113, Wallace Edwards; 114–115, M.P. Kahl/Bruce Coleman Inc., 115, Jane Kurisu; 116, Christian Autotte; 117, Robert Johannsen; 118, Patty Murray/Animals, Animals; 119, Animals, Animals/Oxford Scientific Films, Jonathan Coddington, Dr. T. Eisner; 120–121, Victor Gad; 124, Michael Fogden/ Bruce Coleman Inc.; 126, Jeff Foott/Bruce Coleman Inc.; 128, 134, Jock McRae; 129 Tui De Roy; 130–131, Scott Altenbach; 134–135, Stephen Dalton/NHPA; 136–137, Tom McHugh/Photo Researchers; 138–139, Adrienne Gibson/Animals, Animals; 140–141, Thomas Dannenberg; 142–143, Bruno Kern; 145, Jerry Ferrara; 146, M. Thonig/H. Armstrong Roberts/Miller Services Ltd.; 150–151, Hans Reinhard/Bruce Coleman Inc.; 152–153, John Cancalosi; 154, Elaine Macpherson; 155, Steven Meyers/Animals, Animals; 156, Art Wolfe.